Winter

Val McDermid

WINTER

The Story of a Season

hodder
press

First published in Great Britain in 2025 by Hodder Press
An imprint of Hodder & Stoughton Limited
An Hachette UK company

The authorised representative in the EEA is Hachette Ireland, 8 Castlecourt
Centre, Dublin 15, D15 XTP3, Ireland (email: info@hbgi.ie)

1

Illustrations by Philip Harris

Extract from 'Law of the Island' on p.35 reproduced
with kind permission of Robin Robertson

A CIP catalogue record for this title is available from the British Library

Hardback ISBN 9781399743136
ebook ISBN 9781399743150

Typeset in Sabon MT by Hewer Text UK Ltd, Edinburgh
Printed and bound in Great Britain by Clays Ltd, Elcograf S.p.A.

Hodder & Stoughton policy is to use papers that are natural, renewable
and recyclable products and made from wood grown in sustainable
forests. The logging and manufacturing processes are expected to
conform to the environmental regulations of the country of origin.

Hodder & Stoughton Limited
Carmelite House
50 Victoria Embankment
London EC4Y 0DZ

www.hodderpress.co.uk

For Jo, a woman for all seasons

CONTENTS

'WINTER IS COMING'

WHAT THE TREES SAY

A WHILE BACK, FOR SEVERAL YEARS IN A ROW, I MISSED autumn. I always seemed to be on a lengthy book tour, either in America or Australia. I never even got to see the spectacular fall colours in the US, as American book tours consist of a daily round of airports, the downtowns of new cities, identikit hotel rooms and late-night dinners with kindly booksellers. And in Australia, spring was heading into summer.

By the time I got home, it was as if a switch had been flicked while I was out of the room. I'd left at the tail end of summer; I returned to winter. The trees were bare, the earth was hard underfoot, the house martins gone. It was time to break out the down jacket, the woollen scarf and the gloves.

Since those days, I've managed to better arrange things. As a result, I've grown reaccustomed to the gradual progress from autumn to winter. But, thanks to a particularly wet summer, as this year turned inexorably to winter, the leaves took their time to assume the kaleidoscope of autumn colours, and I've been glad of the panorama of gold and brown, russet and deep scarlet, faded green and pale parchment still clinging to branches, reluctantly revealing the details of their outlines.

The room where I do most of my work has two windows, both with vistas of trees. On one side, mature beeches and silver birches. At night, the fractured bark of the birches' slender white trunks glimmers like ghosts in the darkness, the stray branches of the beech trees giving them the spectral illusion of movement. If I were a character in one of my own novels, I'd be spooked into paranoia by them. Instead, if I'm working late at my desk, I find them curiously calming.

On the other side are old oaks, gnarled and arthritic, a feature of the local nature reserve. I'm not used to seeing so many of them in one place. I grew up in Fife, where James IV ordered all the oaks to be felled for the construction of his vanity project, a warship twice the length of any vessel in the English navy. A new dockyard had to be built at Newhaven specifically to accommodate the ship-building of the *Great Michael*. She was the largest ship afloat until Henry VIII, piqued at being outdone by the Scots, commissioned the *Great Harry*. It was on board the *Great Michael* that the Auld Alliance between France and Scotland was formalised. After that massacre of the oaks, somehow the stock never quite recovered in Fife, so for me, the old oaks are strangers that never cease to please me. In winter, the first frosts produce the crunching underfoot of the pericarps left behind after the acorns have been plundered by squirrels, a percussive counterpoint to the susurration of the fallen leaves.

Seen from my desk, the branches and twigs form a kind of road map. Tracing their paths is the perfect mindless activity when I need to let the wheels turn so the next piece of prose can form in my head. Winter makes it easy to follow strange tracks in my mind; summer is less straightforward, obscured by green.

THE SENSES OF WINTER

I'VE ALWAYS HAD A SOFT SPOT FOR WINTER. FOR MOST people, winter is the poor relation of the seasons. It's not got the fresh excitement of spring, that thrust of new life bursting through the earth, leaves covering barren branches with fleshy crowns in myriad shades of green. It's not got the glamour of summer, when gaudy flowers bloom, people don their bright shirts and skirts and shorts, and streets and parks and beaches are full of the golden light of long days. It's not got the melancholy splendour of autumn, with its mists and mellow fruitfulness, and its cascades of gold and brown, perfect for scuffing through on pavements and paths.

For most people, winter means short days and harsh weather and nipping cold and clothes that disguise us. It's tinged with the longing for warmth and light and escape.

Outside, the cold bites our faces and sneaks in around the cuffs of our gloves and jackets. It reminds me of childhood – knees chapped with cold and legs rubbed raw from the tops of wellies; stamping on ice-covered puddles to release the water beneath the sharp shards; running home from school through rain and sleet and fog for a steaming plate of soup. I even forgive the promise betrayed by those amazing bright blue days when the low sun dazzles me and lulls me into stripping off my scarf and gloves. It's a chance to envelop myself in merino layers, big jumpers and thick socks.

We deal with the hostile environment ('No such thing as bad weather, just the wrong clothes,' as the sanctimonious outdoor-wear marketing managers tell us), then we turn our backs and go inside to the enveloping warmth. It's the time to snuggle indoors without guilt; to curl up on the sofa with a good book or a box set, a hot drink or a wee whisky to hand.

That's not to say that winter should be shrugged off as trivial. As climate change begins to bite, we've had to learn to accept more and worse storms. I was about to go onstage at an event in Dundee when a raucous siren blared through the theatre, every phone in the place sounding the alarm, even those that had been dutifully turned off as instructed by the stage manager. It was a government-issued red alert for Storm Eowyn, ravaging

Ireland first before arriving to devastate central Scotland and northern England. We were warned to stay indoors, not to drive, to be prepared for power cuts.

At the bottom of our garden is a burn, whose headwaters were so churned by the storm that it resembled something belonging to Willy Wonka – a molten milk chocolate stream flowing faster and deeper than I'd ever seen before. The trees on the bank opposite swayed and danced in the wind; some of them are clad in ancient ivy and their movements reminded me of Treebeard, the Lord of the Ents in the Lord of the Rings trilogy. I half-expected them to launch themselves across the burn and march up the garden and across the road to join the old oaks in the nature reserve.

We felt safe inside, but for many people it was a terrifying and destructive experience. Friends posted dramatic photographs of Hokusai-sized waves breaking over harbour walls, of roofs torn off garden sheds and shattered pantiles, fractured red shards vivid against tarmac. And, of course, trampolines liberated from gardens to roll down streets and across railway lines.

And the next day, the wind dropped and the sun shone. As if the weather shrugged and said, 'What? I was just showing off.'

But I love winter precisely because it's Janus-faced. It's nature's equivalent of what the poet Hugh MacDiarmid called the Caledonian antisyzygy – the yoking together of opposing forces. He characterised Scottish nature as composed equally of stern, forbidding Presbyterianism and the dancing, musical, wildness of the Gaels. Dr Jekyll versus Mr Hyde.

It suits me because I am a crime writer. I deal in devious deeds done in the dark. I don't think it's any coincidence that the places where the shortest days last longest have such rich veins of *noir* fiction. *Noir*, after all, speaks of the physical dark as well as the psychological. When in the 1990s Scottish writers began to produce a very distinctive school of hard-bitten crime writing notable for its urban settings and its fascination with violent murder, corruption and black humour, it was only a matter of time before it was christened 'tartan noir' by James Ellroy, an American master of noir.

It's probably also no coincidence that for me, winter is the chosen season of creativity. Once the wild pleasures of the New Year are past, I settle at my desk and write that year's novel. I write my way through those days of scant daylight, revelling in the long shadows that spread themselves out even at noon. The shafts of light that come with occasional splashy dawns and vivid sunsets – not to mention the dazzling curtains of colour from the aurora of the Northern Lights – never keep the darkness at bay for long.

THE DEAD OF WINTER

WHEN THE YEAR TURNS, I SHARPEN MY PENCILS AND FIND the notebook(s) with the scribbled jottings that I've previously made that have some vague connection to what I'm planning to write. I say 'notebook(s)' because those apparently random entries are seldom captured within the covers of one alone. Sometimes they're detailed notes from research I've conducted, often in the National Library of Scotland, but other times in different hushed spaces where strangers are undertaking their own investigations. I always feel like a fraud; I think all those other readers are doing 'proper' research into significant academic topics, whereas I'm likely to be investigating what was showing at the cinema during one particular week in 1989, which albums were in the charts and how much a can of lager cost in a supermarket chain that no longer exists.

Sometimes, the notes I scrawl are incomprehensible to me, even a few days later. When I was researching the mid-air explosion of Pan Am flight 103 over the Scottish Borders town of Lockerbie in December 1988 for my novel *1989*, I was trying to square the contemporary media accounts with my own memories of reporting on that terrible night and its aftermath. But I may not have had the usual emotional distance I seek when I'm mining archives for those nuggets that ignite a spark in my mind and lead me to unanticipated narrative gold. A few days later, when I came to write that section of the book, I struggled to decipher what I'd jotted down.

One line seemed to read 'a whole red cabbage', which made no sense at all. I finally contextualised it and realised it was 'a whole street ablaze'. No wonder I never scored more than a C for handwriting in my primary school report cards.

Thus the notebook that accompanies me on my bus ride to the library is a principal source but never the only one. There'll be at least one other, stuffed into a tote bag or my leather satchel. And a pocket-sized one that comes with me when I leave the house for a walk or a visit to a coffee shop to have a think. Individually, none of them contains much, often nothing more than the name for a character that seems appropriate, or a suggestion of a location where a scene or a story strand might take place.

Then there's the one that lives in my backpack and comes on longer trips, when I travel to festivals or other book events. I always prefer train travel – flying is too bitty and involves hanging around in busy airports where there are too many distractions. I tend to use train journeys for what I think of as figuring out the things I didn't know I was going to need to know. For example, the notebook pages for *Still Life*, a DCI Karen Pirie cold case novel, include such gnomic lines as 'French foreign legion?' 'Transferable band instruments?' 'YBA – prices peaked?' 'Where on Anglesey best for suicide?' 'European extradition warrants – need to talk to a lawyer for process, who do I know who will know?'

IF ON A WINTER'S NIGHT, A TRAVELLER . . .

THERE IS SOMETHING QUITE MAGICAL ABOUT TRAIN travel through a dark landscape. There are so few clues as to where we are. A sudden stream of light flashes past out of nowhere with the promise of strange mysteries; a range of hills is rendered unfamiliar, black on blue; a darkling river glints briefly alongside. Anything could happen while we're cocooned in our carriages and we'd be none the wiser. It's a romance on rails.

I'm always pleased when my diary means I have to take the sleeper to London, particularly in winter. It feels exotic and mysterious to arrive in the capital in the dark, while it's still waking up. I have my regular routine: I check in to my cabin, dump my bag then walk back down the platform to the Club Car for a miniature of Scotch malt whisky. Back at the cabin with my drink, I get ready for bed, smoosh a wee bit of water into the whisky and settle down with my book until we start moving. Then it's lights out and soon I'm rocked to sleep.

One December around the turn of the millennium, I was sent on a book tour in Russia in a joint venture between my UK publisher, my Russian wholesaler and the British Council. My very first novel, *Report for Murder*, had finally been published in Russian a dozen years after its UK debut. It was the first novel ever published officially in Russian with a lesbian protagonist (though obviously there had been *samizdat* publications) and it had gone straight into the bestseller list at number three, much to my astonishment.

The night we heard the news, we were booked on a night train from Moskovsky Station in St Petersburg to Moscow. We started in the restaurant car, drinking vodka to celebrate the book's success. Even as we left, the snow was whirling, a confusion of white against the lace curtains of the carriage, the city's lights an eerie smudge in the background.

After a few drinks and toasts, we headed for our cabins. Walking back through the train, I looked out at a sky emptying fat flakes onto an already white landscape. I imagined a fur-clad Cossack on horseback, galloping through the snow, a rose in his teeth, preparing to draw level and throw it to his lover aboard the train. Absurd, but also irresistible.

There were no roses in my cabin, of course. As so often in Russia, I felt I'd slipped back in time. The bedspread was a multi-coloured crocheted blanket in the style my gran had made by the dozen in my youth, her arthritic fingers working the crochet hook and remnants of wool as she watched TV or gossiped with her pals. She donated them 'for the old folks' well into her seventies. I drifted into sleep to the combination of nostalgia, the music of the train wheels and the swirl of the snow just visible through the tiny window.

I woke at four in the morning, shaken out of sleep by the train juddering to a halt. I couldn't see anything from my cabin but undifferentiated white, so I pulled on some clothes and ventured into the corridor. It reminded me of the star-studded film of *Murder on the Orient Express* and I half-expected Hercule Poirot's moustaches to make an appearance. I stumbled to the vestibule at the end of the carriage and peered out, hoping we were not stuck in a drift like the passengers in Agatha Christie's novel.

The snow had eased and as I peered through the scatter of flakes, I realised we were at a station. An empty platform covered in fresh snow sat between us and our mirror image – another motionless train steaming in the wintry night. As I watched, I saw a couple of men, heads covered in thick caps with earflaps, bodies swathed in railway uniform great-coats, trudging from our train towards the other. Halfway there, they were met by another pair who had left the second train. They paused for a few words, then swapped sides. A few minutes later, we were on our way again.

As I slipped back into sleep, I realised the drivers changed trains at the halfway point of the journey so they could return to their point of departure, finishing back where they started, able to head back to their own beds after a long shift struggling to see the track ahead through the snow. For them, the end of another prosaic night driving a locomotive. For me, an unforgettable winter night.

NOTES TOWARDS
A CONCLUSION

A FEW YEARS AGO, AGATHA CHRISTIE'S FAMILY FOUND boxes in the attic containing seventy-three of her notebooks that had never been examined. They duly hired a Christie expert to decipher them then shared his discoveries in a fascinating book. I appreciated the insight into her mind and method, but I particularly liked the fact that her notebooks resembled mine. Two pages of notes about characters in a novel; a list of spring bulbs to be bought; a few lines about a place that she wanted to use in a book; a plot outline over several pages; a grocery list; a comment about a book she was reading. The editor of the notebooks observed that a particular novel must have been in her mind for a long time because it was referred to in several notebooks. 'I don't think so,' I muttered under my breath when I read his conclusion. 'I think it just depended on which handbag she had with her.'

And so, in the first week of January, I sit down at my desk as I do every year and contemplate the scribble of bare trees against the wintry sky and tell myself the scribbles in the notebooks will come together and make a new book. By this point, I'll usually have made a tentative start – a few sentences that I hope will grab my readers' interest.

I've never forgotten the lessons I learned from my first news editor. One was, 'Always go to the loo when you have the chance because you never know when you'll have another opportunity.' Still a useful precept, particularly in winter, but not as relevant to my present working life as, 'Your first paragraph should make them *need* to read on.' I still cleave to that principle, more important than ever these days when there are so many distractions and calls on our diminishing attention spans. I know this to be true; it affects me too, much more than it used to. I can be pulled out of a book that's not doing its job as easily as anyone else. I want to be seduced; I *need* to be seduced or I'll sidle along the shelf, stroking the spines till I find something else to draw me in . . .

The direction of travel of each year's book is established in the first few weeks of January. The weather is invariably inhospitable so there are few temptations to pull me away from the business of crafting those early pages. It goes slowly at first; if all goes well, I manage to get the first fifty pages written by the end of the month.

It's a target I can usually hit and it bolsters me when I do because that's a pattern of production I feel I can rely on. Even after forty novels, I still need the reassurance that my skills haven't melted away during the gap between the end of the previous book and now.

I don't have superstitions. I don't need to swivel my chair round three times widdershins or have a particular brand of new notebook and a special pencil to write in it with. I just get stuck in. I brew a mug of coffee, pull on my felt, fingerless Icelandic mittens, boot up the computer, put on some music – instrumental, often Nordic, mostly as skeletal as the trees – and move slowly forward, one sentence at a time. I feel a bit like a mole, digging through the cold, dark ground with little pink paws. Those first weeks are always much more about rewriting and editing; the first stumbling attempts at seducing my readers.

When the sun shines, though, I let myself be drawn from my desk into the open air. Especially if that air is still and there is frost crisping the grass and the fallen leaves, as it has been this year. Chances are, I'll crunch my way through them and make my way down to the shore, to where the Firth of Forth divides Edinburgh from my native Fife.

Never mind not being able to step into the same river twice; when it comes to the Forth estuary, you can never see the same river twice. Sometimes it's Mediterranean blue, flat, calm and welcoming to swimmers, paddle boarders and kayakers. Other times it broods in dark navy, a muscular swell carrying the tide waters to the North Sea. In winter, it's mostly at least fifty shades of grey, windblown into white horses, high tide attacking harbours and sea walls with spectacular spray. But even in January, there are days when the skies are clear brilliant blue and the sea settles down. Grey seals and harbour seals clamber on to the rocks of the shore platforms, shags perch alongside, spreading their wings wide to dry. If I'm lucky, I might spot a pod of dolphins, a minke whale or even a basking shark, described by the great Scottish poet Norman MacCaig as, 'That roomsized monster with a matchbox brain.'

BRIDGING

I LIKE TO CATCH A BUS TO SOUTH QUEENSFERRY IN winter when it's too cold for the tourists. I wait for one of those clear blue days with a cloudless sky for the best contrasts. Then I peacefully admire the three iconic bridges out in the waters of the Forth, when snow crowns the Ochil Hills on the far shore.

Number one: a UNESCO World Heritage Site that carries dozens of trains a day across the Forth. The first major steel structure in the world, its three diamond-shaped cantilevers in dark red are recognisable the world over. It's at the heart of what many readers consider to be the best novel by Iain Banks, *The Bridge*. The protagonist is driving down the motorway towards the crossing, but he's struck as ever by the beauty of the rail bridge:

> The old rail bridge's hollow metal bones looked the colour of dried blood.

You fucking beauty, he thought . . . What a gorgeous great device you are. So delicate from this distance, so massive and strong close-up. Elegance and grace; perfect form. A quality bridge; granite piers, the best ship-plate steel, and a never-ending paint job . . .

It remains irresistibly at the heart of the book.

And it does feel inescapable. Its image adorns everything from calendars to shortbread tins, from t-shirts to beer cans, from aprons to arms, tattooed as an intricate bracelet. I feel a fragment of ownership: my great-grandfather left his home on the whisky island of Islay to work as a riveter on the bridge. I've scrutinised dozens of old photographs of the work crews on the bridge searching for the McDermid features that so many of my relatives share – round faces, definite noses, long ears and an absence of frown lines. So far, I've not found anyone I can lay claim to. But I keep the small flame of hope alive in my heart.

Number two: the road bridge. A long-span suspension bridge of concrete and steel similar to its big brother, the more glamorous Golden Gate bridge across San Francisco bay. Before its construction, if we wanted to go from Fife to Edinburgh by car, we had to drive to North Queensferry, drive on to an actual ferry and cross over to South Queensferry – never much fun in winter's icy grasp. The only alternative was to add another thirty-five miles to the journey and travel upriver to where the much shorter (and infinitely less glamorous) Kincardine Bridge still stands.

When the road bridge opened in 1964, it was the longest of its kind outside America. When the Queen came to open it officially, I was there with my primary school class to wave my tiny Union flag at her as she drove past. It's not quite a World Heritage Site but it is a Grade A listed structure, and these days it carries a much smaller volume of traffic – public transport, pedestrians and cyclists. It's worth crossing to get the best uninterrupted view of the other two bridges that flank it, but you'd be a brave soul to walk or cycle across on a winter's day with the snell easterly wind scouring its way up the estuary.

And finally, number three: the Queensferry Crossing. It's a slender, graceful cable-stay structure, the longest of its kind in the world. Driving down the motorway towards it, it resembles an enormous, elegant racing yacht under full sail, a ghost ship with frost glittering on its rigging, shining triumphant in the dark like a vast ice sculpture.

Battered by wind and weather, all three of the bridges are a breathtaking sight in a winter storm; lashed by rain, hail, sleet and snow, they feel like impossible survivors.

There's plenty going on under the bridge decks too. Standing on the quayside in South Queensferry, wrapped up against the weather, I can watch cruise ships heading towards Norway and the promise of the Northern Lights;

cabin cruisers off for a weekend away or a day's fishing; oil rigs awaiting refits; crane barges for raising offshore electricity-generating windmills; workhorse tugs and tankers riding at anchor, awaiting their turn upstream at the Grangemouth refinery; tiny fishing boats collecting their crab and lobster pots.

And then there are the islands. Cramond Island is closest to Edinburgh, linked by a tidal causeway. Along with Inchgarvie and Inchmickery, Cramond was a key part of a line of gun emplacements during the Second World War. They had the dual objective of protecting the anti-submarine booms that defended the key infrastructure of the Forth Bridge from underwater attack, and guarding Edinburgh against enemy aircraft. My father was briefly stationed on Inchmickery – briefly because he was only in the Black Watch for 124 days before being discharged. His crime? He lied about his age to volunteer. His two older brothers had already signed up to do their bit in the war and he wanted to be a hero too.

Unfortunately, my grandfather was subsequently sent to jail for black marketeering cigarettes in the naval dockyard at Rosyth. This left my poor grandmother with insufficient income and two younger children still at home. Nevertheless, although registered blind, she was a resourceful woman. She threw herself on the mercy of my father's commanding officer and revealed his true age. I can imagine the poor man was only too happy to release my father from his platoon if only to get rid of my gran, a formidable woman at the best of times. No sooner had she got her wayward son home than she organised a job for him in the shipyard, a reserved occupation that meant he was spared from military service.

Every time I cross the Forth on the train, I can't resist a wry smile at the thought of my father on that barren strip of rock. He wasn't sorry to leave; it had been January, after all. But equally, I can't resist the fantasy of living on Inchmickery. I imagine being alone on the rock, a sort of writer in residence. It wouldn't be peaceful; the trains overhead, the sea assaulting the rock, the cacophony of the birds.

So where would my imagination go then? Nobody to talk to but those amazing birds. Fulmars, razorbills, guillemots, all with their curiously prehistoric heads. And, of course, the gannets soaring overhead with their wide wingspans, white bodies and wings with jet black tips, the yellow of their neck feathers resembling warheads plummeting into the waves like heat-seeking missiles, utterly intent on their prey. Their beauty is terrifying when you see them close up. Beaks like skewers and beady black eyes to match. I'm drawn to them but ever since I read Robin Robertson's poem 'Law of the Island' I'm also petrified at their potential. Read it and tremble:

They lashed him to old timbers
that would barely float,
with weights at the feet so
only his face was out of the water.
Over his mouth and eyes
they tied two live mackerel
with twine, and pushed him
out from the rocks.
They stood, then,
smoking cigarettes
and watching the sky,
waiting for a gannet
to read that flex of silver
from a hundred feet up,
close its wings
and plummet-dive.

It'd be a relief to escape my imagination and return to either shore, to the *peep peep peep* of the oyster catchers, the awkward stride of the curlew, those show-off cormorants with their drying wings. But it would be an adventure. An adventure for summer, though. Not winter.

This year, however, there will be far fewer seabirds, gannets included. Avian flu has taken a heavy toll. Their raucous colony on the Bass Rock out in the Forth, the most populous gannetry in the world, has received a particularly terrible blow. Last winter, walking a section of the Fife Coastal Path a mere mile and a half long, we passed a dozen dead. Some looked as if they were sleeping. Others had their necks stretched as if they were reaching for elusive air. The word is that the disease has run its course, but nobody feels entirely confident.

It's not always the obvious that is the source of danger for the birds. On Craigleith, famous for its puffin colony of ten thousand breeding pairs, the population of what is undeniably the cutest and most comedic of all seabirds fell in a few short years by 90 per cent because of tree mallows, giant invasive plants whose roots make it impossible for the birds to dig the burrows where they incubate their eggs and raise their young. Ever since the calamitous fall in numbers, volunteers have been working to eradicate the mallows. In spite of the efforts of more than a thousand supporters of the puffins, the mallows persist, though their numbers have been reduced sufficiently to allow the puffins to start rebuilding their colonies. They're a welcome sight; it would be a hard heart that didn't feel a rise in its spirit at the sight of a puffin.

TALKING TO MY SELVES

NO MATTER WHICH SIDE OF THE WIDE ESTUARY I'M walking beside, I'll be trying out the conversations my characters need to have next. The rhythm of the waves and the rhythm of my steps provokes the different cadences of their speech in my head. Sometimes the words escape from the inside of my head and without intending to, I start muttering the more intense verbal exchanges. I only realise it's happening when passers-by give me strange looks or a wide berth. Or the look of recognition that goes, 'Oh, it's her, that writer, pay her no mind, she'll be in a world of her own.'

I relish in particular walking through the bright blue days; they feel like a gift in the dead of dreichness and provide an opportunity for resolving thorny scenes where characters are at odds with each other. Or with me. It's not that characters have a life of their own – it's that the life I have given them, the personalities and life choices, do not always permit me to squeeze them into the course of action I think they need to take. So, as the French say, I have to *reculer pour mieux sauter* – take some steps backwards to take another run at the problem. Often, solutions fall into place on those shoreline wanderings, washed up like so much driftwood.

And then I return to my cosy office and see if those conversations work as well on the page as they have on my lips. That contrast with the outside world is reassuring but it also provokes some twinges of guilt for me.

When I was a teenager, I played guitar and sang in folk clubs, first at school and then in any pubs and clubs into which I could bluff my under-age way for the open mic section of the evening. In Kirkcaldy, where we lived, there was an excellent folk club in the Elbow Room pub. The thriving folk scene in Scotland meant we had a regular roll call of top names, from Billy Connolly to Barbara Dickson. One of the regulars was the hugely talented Rab Noakes, a phenomenal guitarist and prolific songwriter who worked with Gerry Rafferty and, among others, the chart-topping Newcastle band Lindisfarne. It was that connection that opened up a new consciousness that has remained part of my life.

Like Rab, Lindisfarne's lead singer was also a talented songwriter. And one of his songs knocked me back on my heels. I'd started to develop a political awareness in my teens, rooted in the left-of-centre views of my parents and grandparents. We were working class but although we never had much money to spare, we always had a roof over our heads, food on the table and coal on the fire – one of the few benefits of working underground hewing coal. I don't think I'd thought much beyond that.

Then one night Rab Noakes stepped up to the mic. He was in his early twenties back then, the nearest we had to a heartthrob on the Fife folk scene. Luxuriant brown hair, chiselled good looks, a slightly goofy smile as he adjusted his guitar tuning. Knitted woollen polo neck, flared jeans, Cuban-heeled boots – every inch the folk singer. I could imagine him walking the highway with a scarf trailing down his back, guitar case in hand, a flurry of snow blurring his outline, a new set of lyrics taking shape behind his eyes.

I learned so much from Rab and the other performers at the Elbow Room. I watched and memorised the restless fingers of their left hands on the fretboard and studied the licks and fingerpicking they used with their right. I'd store it away and practise for hours back in my bedroom. I saw how they put a song across to an audience and stole the tricks of their trade for myself. Over the years, I parlayed those tricks into drinks, money and romantic encounters.

And I learned their songs too. Everything from traditional murder ballads like 'Twa Corbies' to Carole King's 'You've Got a Friend', via the dark obscurity of Leonard Cohen and Bob Dylan. But in spite of the place those tracks have in my heart, the song that completely changed my view of the world was 'Winter Song', written by Lindisfarne's front man, Alan Hull.

His lines spoke passionately about the contrast between our comfortable lives and the tribulations of those for whom winter was a gruelling battle for survival – for homeless people struggling in freezing temperatures to stay alive; for travellers with no security, spurned and insulted, and driven off the land by court edicts. Alan Hull reminds his listeners of the parallels with Jesus, 'Who got busted just for talking / and befriending the wrong sorts,' a couplet that has fresh resonances for us now with the current attitudes to protest.

Sometimes a song will strike straight to the heart and 'Winter Song' did that for me. It made me sad and angry, emotions that were only reinforced when, soon afterwards, I heard Ralph McTell's equally eloquent 'Streets of London'. It dawned on me that the glamorous lifestyle I'd painted in my head for one of my folksinger friends was nothing of the sort.

I'd got to know Big Jim McHarg from our school folk club, where he was a regular guest performer. He was always on the move, from town to town, from gig to gig, nothing to tie him down but a rucksack and a guitar case. It seemed like a romantic life to me, free from ties and constraint, his own boss, able to go wherever he pleased. He was talented, that much was obvious as soon as he started to play. And he was generous with his skills. I remember him spending most of one afternoon teaching me how to play 'Angie', a complex and demanding instrumental. I never managed it at full speed but that I could manage it at all was down to Big Jim.

He died of a heroin overdose in the winter of 1971 when I was sixteen.

I realised from what emerged then that he'd been one of the hidden homeless that 'Winter Song' had been about. Big Jim, I discovered, had been what we now call a sofa surfer, scrounging a bed for the night after every gig. Mostly, he was lucky because he was good company as well as a good performer, and people felt almost honoured to put him up and feed him breakfast before he headed off for his next gig. And his next fix, as it turned out. But sometimes, he'd be forced to sleep in bus shelters and train stations.

Knowing that Alan Hull's lyrics reflected the real life of someone I'd known changed me.

A few years later, I was an undergraduate at Oxford, where winter is cold and damp, miserable vapours from the rivers shrouding the dreaming spires, covering shoulders and hair with tiny droplets of water. I longed for a Fife winter with its bitter clarity; damp eats into my very soul. The occasional day of watercolour blue skies felt nothing like vivid enough. There were whole weeks at a time when I never felt properly dry or properly warm. Imagine being homesick for crisp cold . . .

I was loosely attached to a shifting group of fellow undergraduates who gathered for coffee after dinner in someone's college room. One night, a friend of a friend started talking about a barge on the canal that was a support centre for homeless people. It was run by a charity called Cyrenians, and it provided hot drinks and food to people struggling with life on the street. I remembered the vivid impact Alan Hull's song had had on me and realised this might offer a way to do something useful.

I became a volunteer, turning up once a week to brew tea and sit down with homeless men and women and listen to their stories. I don't know what they made of my callow attempts at understanding, but at least for a brief time, they were warm and dry and fed. It was an experience that has stayed with me; in winter, it's where my thoughts often turn.

I still replicate that small service when I can. Over the years, I've been told time and time again not to give money to people who are living on the streets. I understand why we're given that injunction even if it does feel, deep down, as if I'm dismissing their autonomy. And so when it's possible, I buy them a hot drink. And I support charities that support them. Still, it shames me that half a century on from my first encounter with homeless people, they're still freezing to death on the streets of one of the richest countries in the world.

'GIVE US BREAD, BUT GIVE US ROSES'

PARTY TIME

IN SPITE OF THE CHALLENGES OF THE SEASON, IT'S undeniable that all the best festivals are in winter – Hallowe'en and the Samhuinn fire festival, Diwali, Bonfire Night, St Andrew's Night, Saturnalia with its misrule and role inversion, Christmas, Hogmanay, Burns Night, Up Helly Aa . . .

Some might argue that summer trumps this with Glastonbury, the Edinburgh festivals, Boardmasters, Green Man and the like. But those festivals are exclusive. You have to have money for tickets and the patience to queue to buy them. Then there's the cost of travel and accommodation, and exposure to food that will likely send your digestive tract into shock.

Conversely, winter's festivals are accessible to all. Of course, there are optional extras that will make a dent in your wallet. But the key word is 'optional'. You can lean into tradition and do the winter festivals on a shoestring.

And in winter, we need something to take our minds off the privations of the season. Summer's a flibberti-gibbet; as Robert Burns says, its pleasures are like poppies spread. It's easy to find lovely distractions. Winter makes greater demands on us. We're muffled up in woolly jumpers and big boots, raincoats are never enough to keep us warm for long, and we lose the light so quickly that even simple pleasures like a woodland walk are constrained by the early dark. Rain, snow, fog, ice, drizzle and bitter winds conspire against our best intentions. That's why we embrace whatever excess we can find.

For me, the proper start of winter has always been Hallowe'en. Some might argue it's an autumn festival, but I grew up in Fife, on the east coast of Scotland, and by the end of October, the sun was disappearing below the horizon by the time I got home from school. I had my duffel coat over my blazer, my scarf tucked around my neck, my hands muffled in woollen mittens. The only light in the gathering gloom was Hallowe'en and the build-up lasted most of the month. We needed something to remind us that the light always comes back!

Like most of my friends, I spent October making my plans for guising. Guising is the forerunner of the anae-mic trick or treat that Scots kids now indulge them-selves with. The ancient tradition of guising crossed the Atlantic to the US and succumbed to simplification and commercialisation.

Back when we went guising, the notion of buying a costume would never have crossed our minds. Apart from anything else, there were no Hallowe'en costumes on sale. No witches' outfits with pointed hats and stick-on warts; no skeleton suits with dramatic plastic cobwebs; no Count Draculas with billowing cloaks and bloody fangs. We had to improvise.

In 1962, for example, I owned a large orange sombrero made from moulded cardboard pulp. It had been given to me at a kids' Christmas party and I'd clung on to it as a prop for my imagination. *The Lone Ranger* was fuel for my lurid fantasies; the concept of cultural appropriation hadn't arrived in Fife in the 1960s.

Pat Boone's 'Speedy Gonzales' was a chart hit that year and I was captivated by the strangulated falsetto that opened the song. I drove my mother mad as I ran about the house singing along with the music that was in my head. It was a no-brainer that this would be my Hallowe'en party piece. My poor mother gave in and found an old burnt-orange curtain, cut a hole for my head and all I needed then was a belt, for the simplest guising costume ever.

The following year, when I was eight, my costume was inspired by my father's mysterious acquisition of a bowler hat. There was no explanation for its appearance on one of the clothes pegs in the hall; it simply arrived out of the blue. I wonder now whether he'd knocked it off the head of an Orangeman to show his disdain for sectarianism, but at the time, he never explained it. I never saw him wear it either. At some later point it disappeared, also without comment. I didn't pay attention to its departure; by that time it had served its purpose.

It wasn't enough to chap on someone's door and demand, 'Trick or treat!' If we wanted a reward, we didn't threaten. We had to sing for our supper. As well as dressing up to impersonate a recognisable figure, we had to perform – ideally a schtick connected to the figure we were imitating. In my case, that year, the chart-topping clarinettist Acker Bilk was my disguise.

As well as his trademark bowler hat, I wore a white school shirt, a waistcoat borrowed from my cousin's formal Highland dress outfit and a pair of black nylon skating pants. My mum scraped some soot from the fireplace and drew on Acker Bilk's moustache and goatee. I didn't have a clarinet, obviously. But I did have a bagpipe chanter, which was the right size and if you half-closed your eyes on a dark doorstep might just about have passed muster. So when unsuspecting neighbours opened their doors, I would lift the chanter to my mouth and croon the instantly recognisable hit 'Stranger on the Shore'.

I had with me the other essential accessory for guising – the turnip lantern, the predecessor of the American pumpkin lantern. When pumpkins began to appear over here as a supposed source for lanterns, we regarded them with utter contempt. This was guising for softies. Gouging the rock-hard raw flesh out of a large swede (or neep, as we said in Fife, definitely not rutabaga, as Americans choose to call them) required strength and persistence. Even as I type these words, my hands twinge with the memory of pain.

In my family, one of our traditions was stealing the turnip from the field of a farmer near my grandparents' house. Under cover of darkness, three or four of us would crawl along the hedgerow bordering the neep field looking out for prize specimens. The top half of the swede protrudes from the earth, a dark reddish-purple hemisphere with an erect crown of green leaves. It wasn't hard to pull them free from the fine loam of the Fife soil, revealing the pale orange-tinged root. We'd run all the way home with our booty, terrified the farmer would chase us. He never did, but he might have . . .

Back home, washed clean of soil, the bottom of the root was chopped off to make a stable base. Then the top got the same treatment to form the lid. Next, the excavation began. Under my father's guidance, I'd use a mallet and a chisel to carve chunks of the orange flesh out of the vegetable. My mother would salvage them to cook as accompaniment to the next day's dinner.

Eventually, my father would judge I'd made enough inroads into the swede to carve its face. This was the point where he took over. Using a craft knife, he'd cut two triangles for eyes, another, longer and narrower, for a nose, then a jagged sliver of moon for a mouth, with broken matchsticks for teeth. My mother would produce a candle from the supply kept under the sink in case of power cuts. She'd light it and shoogle it around till there was enough melted wax to hold it upright. Even if we'd known about tealights in their little metal cups, I suspect we'd have scoffed at them for not doing it right.

Finally, my father would take a bradawl and make two holes near the top of the neep and two in the lid. I'd thread string through them so the lid could sit tight while I carried the lantern. To this day the smell of burning turnip transports me in space and time like Proust's madeleine.

Off I went into the damp chill October night, one or two of my pals at my side, our breath clouds in the air, the acrid smell of coal smoke from chimneys tantalising us with the promise of warm living rooms. We knocked on the doors of everyone we knew in the surrounding streets – and those of a few of the scary or creepy older folk who habitually tutted at us in the street – and announced we were the guisers. Some kept us on the doorstep performing our hearts out, but mostly we were invited into living rooms we'd never glimpsed before. Posh (English) Mrs Norman; grumpy Miss Michie; aggressive Mr Fergusson, domesticated as a neutered ginger tom by the presence of his wife, and the Polish Maleks with their interesting wall hangings and Catholic images.

Even then, I was curious about other people's lives. I was a voracious reader already, and living across the street from the central library had only fuelled my fascination. The window on other lives, I now understand, was even more of a bonus than the money and sweets that our audiences gave us.

And there were the parties my gran threw on the Friday nearest Hallowe'en. My maternal grandparents lived in East Wemyss, a mining village eight miles away from Kirkcaldy, and I stayed overnight with them on Fridays so my parents could indulge their favourite pastime of attending a dinner dance at a local hotel; they loved getting dressed up and spending an evening on the dance floor, waltzing the working week into memory.

So I had two sets of pals: my schoolmates during the week, my Wemyss pals on a weekend and school holidays. My Wemyss pals were always welcome in my grandparents' house. Unlike my mother, who thought children made the house cluttered and untidy, my gran was relaxed about a bunch of kids turning their small flat upside down. Her Hallowe'en parties were the stuff of legend. We'd all turn up in our guising outfits, the air thick with the smell of singed neeps, and get ready for messy games.

First there was dooking for apples. Gran filled the washing up bowl with water and tipped a bag of apples into it. One by one, we kneeled on the floor next to it and, hands tied behind our backs with a scarf, we had to retrieve a floating apple by biting into it. Sounds easy enough, right? Just give it a try next time you want to get soaked to the skin from the waist up . . .

Then there were treacle scones. My gran would bake a batch of scones then cut them in half. She'd thread a darning needle with wool and pull it through the scone. Then she'd lower the pulley – the ceiling-mounted clothes airer – and tie the end of the wool to it so the scones were at head height for us kids. Sheets of newspaper would be placed on the floor. The final piece of preparation for the ordeal was to spread the scone with black treacle or golden syrup.

Then, again with our hands tied behind our backs, we had to eat the dripping scone. Anyone who succeeded would be rewarded with a lucky tattie – a traditional

Scottish confection designed to vaguely resemble sauté potatoes, consisting of flat discs of fondant flavoured with cinnamon and sprinkled with the powdered spice.

Just in case we hadn't had enough sugar, the games were followed by toffee apples, treacle toffee and tablet, the Scottish tooth-rotting treat made from sugar, condensed milk and butter. Similar to fudge, only sweeter . . .

I loved Hallowe'en.

That love of the festival that ushers in winter and whose lanterns banish the dark followed me into adulthood. A few years ago, we were invited to a lavish party on Hallowe'en. We had to dress up, but not in our finery. Instead, we were instructed to wear fancy dress that represented our worst nightmare. We pondered long and hard over this, discarding the obvious aliens, bad fairies, witches and ghouls. We discussed whether our worst nightmare was internal or external and eventually we decided we were more unnerved by what we might turn into rather than what might attack us.

We decided our worst nightmare and greatest shame would be to turn into Perthshire Tories in all their respectable *petit bourgeois* glory.

We plundered the local charity shops and Primark. Jo, my partner, invested in a joke shop Marilyn Monroe wig that she backcombed and stiffened with hairspray. Blue eyeshadow, red lipstick, tartan pencil skirt, pink polyester blouse and a string of fake pearls rendered her unrecognisable. She looked like the bastard love child of Myra Hindley and Margaret Thatcher.

I opted for black capris tucked into pink argyle-patterned socks, pink shirt and a tank top in knock-off Pringle style. Plus an inflatable golf club and blue suede Oxford brogues. I flattened my silver hair, gave it a side parting and added a stick-on moustache. I bore a worrying resemblance to Scottish comic actor Ford Kiernan, star of *Still Game*.

We made the right choice – we were voted the winners on the night. Definitely a triumph for the traditional guisers!

Hallowe'en shares 31 October with Samhuinn, celebrated in Edinburgh with a spectacular fire festival in the shadow of Arthur's Seat, the extinct volcano that looms above the heart of the city. It starts with a thrumming crescendo of drums that vibrates in our chests, flaming torches endangering anyone with too much hairspray or man-made fabrics. Then we're treated to a dramatic display of fire play and breathtaking acrobatics to mark the changing of the seasons. The air is thick with smoke and the smell of burning torches. It feels utterly primitive – all the more so for taking place within sight of the ultra-modern Scottish Parliament building and Holyrood House, a royal palace since the twelfth century.

And that feeling is right on the money. For the Samhuinn we watch now is a modern reimagining of an ancient pagan tradition that has at its heart the epic battle between summer and winter as the year's wheel turns. We gaze in amazement at participants playing the roles of bizarre creatures from both worlds and the space between them. Imagine a cast of characters let loose in the costume departments of *Lord of the Rings, Braveheart* and *Dracula* and you'll get the picture – kilts and cloaks, furs and headdresses, faces painted white and blood red. The final confrontation comes between the two costumed queens of the warring seasons, while the Cailleach, the one-eyed hag who brings winter and storms, drags us away from light and warmth into the dark nights and the cold days of winter.

Of course, the energetic conflict of the night, striking though it is, can never be more than a spectacle. We all know that however hard the summer royalty fight, the Cailleach will triumph and summer will be cast out. For me, that lack of suspense always cuts through the excitement of the night; just for once, it would be truly exciting to see the world turned upside down and for summer to chase winter away. Instead, we have to wait for the natural order to re-emerge at the Beltane festival at the end of

April, when summer is allowed to return and drive winter back into the shadows. The only real victory to celebrate at Samhainn is the transitional shift as the trees change colour, animals prepare for hibernation and the migratory birds exchange their respective positions. Most of us don't even have fires to light at home any longer.

GUNPOWDER,
TREASON AND PLOT

IF I WAS A DIFFERENT KIND OF WRITER, I'D REVEL IN imagining the counterfactual of what would have happened in Scotland if Guy Fawkes and his cohort of conspirators had succeeded in blowing up the English Parliament in 1605. The Union of the Crowns, joining the thrones of Scotland and England under one monarch, had taken place only two years before; it would still have been relatively simple for Scotland to have disengaged and continue to run its own affairs under its own laws . . .

But that's not what happened, so less than a week after Hallowe'en and Samhuinn's flames and drumbeats, it's time for a different celebration of fire – Bonfire Night. As a child, I was familiar with the celebration of Guy Fawkes' attempt to blow up the Houses of Parliament, if not with the politics of it. The attempted coup had been the subject of comic books, classroom tales and even a skipping rhyme:

> Please to remember
> The fifth of November;
> Gunpowder, treason and plot!
> I know of no reason
> Why the Gunpowder Treason
> Should ever be forgot!

It was a tale of derring-do and excitement, unmediated by the actual history surrounding the event. I was well into my twenties before it dawned on me that its 1605 roots lay in English anti-Catholic sentiment stoked by King James I and VI.

The destruction of the Houses of Parliament was meant to be the first blow in a revolution to replace the king with his daughter Elizabeth – already betrothed to the Catholic King of France at the age of only nine – in a bid to generate more religious tolerance. Or at least, a different flavour of savage bigotry. Epic fail, and still sectarian bigotry mars our society.

Hard to believe, I know, but back in the olden days of my childhood, there was only one TV channel that screened adverts. And it broadcast in monochrome. During every ad break between Hallowe'en and Bonfire

Night, we held our breath as the Standard Fireworks jingle rang out – 'Light up the sky with Standard Fireworks!' The screen filled with vivid starbursts of imagined colour, then panned back to show wide-eyed small children mouthing, 'Ooh,' and 'Aah.'

Every household in our street that included children lit up their own corner of the sky with fireworks to celebrate Guy Fawkes. Everyone had their own favourites among the selection boxes that appeared in the days after Hallowe'en. Roman Candle, Golden Rain, Jack in the Box, Rainbow Fountain, Volcano, the Catherine Wheel that never spun around no matter how carefully the nail was hammered into a fence post, and my least favourite, the boring Chrysanthemum Fountain that sprayed a fan of yellow sparks, short in both spectacle and duration. But I loved sparklers – the joy of writing names and even messages that burned on the retina for seconds then disappeared forever. Capering round our tiny back garden with a brilliant writing stick remains one of the high-lights of my winter memories.

My dad took charge on Bonfire Night. Mere women and children couldn't be trusted with the glowing taper that ignited the individual fireworks once they'd been placed securely on the ground. Of course we couldn't! We never questioned that, until the year he tripped over a stone and dropped the taper in the box.

For a brief instant, it looked as if he might pluck it out in time but it was too late. At least one blue touch paper was lit and, within seconds, the whole box was aflame. A cacophony of bangs and screaming whistles, rainbows of colour flying in all directions, a spectacular I'd never dreamed of. It lasted less than a minute, fizzling out in a literal display of a damp squib.

That was the last time we had our own fireworks. After that, we spent Bonfire Night in the garden of a neighbour who actually built a bonfire. Most of the street pitched up and donated their own boxes of fireworks to the common display. It made for far too many Chrysanthemum Fountains, but, as a compensation, there were always a couple of dads who splashed out on big rockets that climbed high over the rooftops and detonated with a satisfying bang and a scream and a comet trail of coloured sparks.

Best of all were the potatoes and sausages wrapped in tinfoil and placed round the outside of the bonfire. As the evening wore on, the smell of fireworks was replaced by the unmistakable aroma of the singeing skins of baked potatoes. Eventually, the flames died down enough for the food to be salvaged from the ashes. Nothing ever tasted better to my childhood palate than those blackened potatoes and sausages.

Back home, pets cowered whimpering under tables.

Our dog tried to squeeze under the sofa, my mother soothing him with a steady supply of doggy chocs. With the unthinking cruelty of children, I think we mostly felt scorn rather than sympathy for the poor terrified beasts. Years later, though, I had a cat who loved fireworks. She'd push the curtain aside to perch on the windowsill and stare out at the sky, untroubled by the bangs and whistles. I felt ridiculously proud of her.

Now, firework displays are mostly municipal events. Officially and efficiently organised, with health and safety to the fore, and no active participation by the audience. But still, on patches of waste ground and derelict car parks where bin fires are often more common, the tradition persists of local lads – and it is mostly lads – spending the weeks leading up to Bonfire Night gathering any wood they can get their hands on. Pallets filched from the back doors of warehouses, broken furniture tossed to the kerbside, the random products of skip diving. The fire itself is constructed as carefully and cunningly as any of the council's Building Service division could manage. And then it has to be protected from rival predators. There's nothing casual or feckless about the preservation of the perfectly balanced pyre. Reputations are at stake; some bonfire crews even run night shift rotas to take care of their constructions, especially if they're topped by an effigy of a local hate figure – usually a politician or a footballing rival.

Edinburgh is a city addicted to the crash, bang, wallop that goes with the heavenly glamour cascading down Castle Rock from the Esplanade to the gardens below. The city doesn't confine itself to 5 November nor does it wait for winter – on every night of the Edinburgh Military Tattoo during the festival month of August the sound of fireworks reverberates through the city centre.

But Edinburgh saves its most breathtaking spectacles for the Hogmanay celebration. It's visible from the other side of the Firth of Forth, several miles away. We Scots do have a tendency to excess at New Year and the pyromania sets the tone. But more of that later.

RUMMAGE

WINTER MEANS SOUP. I BELIEVE THE WORLD IS DIVIDED in two: those who think soup is a meal and those who are wrong. Of course, it's possible to have a small bowl as a starter, ahead of a main course. In winter when I was growing up, there was always soup with our dinner, a steaming bowl to start the meal. But for real afficionados, a suitably fulsome soup is a meal in itself.

Me, I love soup. Probably because my mother was a fine soup maker. When my godson visited me, he always used to demand Nanna Da's soup, a Scotch broth variant with stock made from boiling beef. The piece of beef is removed before serving, shredded then returned to the bowls when the soup is dished up. But now his partner is a pescatarian, the boiling beef has been consigned to oblivion, replaced by a vegetable stock gel . . . Even the best traditions have to move with the times. But the soup love remains.

When I went off to university, I decided I wanted to make dinner for a few friends to celebrate St Andrew's Night. He is the patron saint of Scotland and 30 November is our national day. We don't make much of a fuss over it, at least not in Scotland itself. But we do give a nod to our winter favourites. I hoped to impress my English friends with the richness of Scottish cuisine. I'd persuaded my mother to send me a haggis in the post but I needed more. I needed soup.

'Can I have your soup recipe?' I asked on one of our occasional phone calls. ('Occasional' because I never had cash to spare to shove in the payphone's greedy maw and my mother was paranoid about losing her low user rebate from the phone company.)

There was a long silence.

'Mum? The recipe?' I prompted her.

'There isnae a recipe,' she said. 'You make a stock with boiling beef or a chicken carcase, then you chop up whatever vegetables you've got, then throw in some lentils and barley and some dried peas or beans, whatever you've got, and a tin of tomatoes if you've got some, tomato puree if not. Then you simmer it for a few hours. It's no' really a recipe, more a rummage.'

In a way, that phone call defined my view of cooking. A recipe is always a starting point; it can invariably be improved by a good rummage then tweaking and adding other ingredients. The perennial cry in our kitchen as one or other of us is stirring a pan is, 'There's a missing middle. I think it needs some balsamic/chipotle/chaat masala/Worcestershire sauce/pickled walnuts.' Nowhere is my tendency to ignore a recipe more evident than in the area of soup.

Family legend has it that as a small child, I announced I didn't like lentil soup. So my mother sneakily added a tin of tomatoes, put the new variant through a sieve and told me it was tomato soup. I was suckered, and sucked in.

Now, I have a repertoire of my own. When we've had shellfish on the barbecue, I gather up the heads and shells and make a rich and fragrant fish stock with garlic – wild garlic when it's in season – and the tops of the fennel plants that self-seed in the garden. I strain the stock, add smoked tomato paste, shallots, a tin of chopped tomatoes and some chilli powder to create a stonking fish soup. A swirl of rouille and some croutons made with the end of the rye sourdough loaf, and I defy anyone to say it's not a meal.

Simplest of all is mushroom soup. Chop a shallot and a couple of cloves of garlic and sweat in some olive oil and butter. Then add a sliced punnet of whatever mushrooms are available. If there are any dried porcini in the cupboard, crumble them, pour on some boiling water, and leave them to infuse before adding to the pan. Add whatever stock you prefer, simmer for half an hour then pulverise with a stick blender. Serve as it comes or add a swirl of crème fraîche if you're feeling the need for a bit of luxury.

One of my favourites is 'bottom of the fridge soup'. The day before the big shop, there are always bits and pieces. Rub the sprouting bits and eyes out of the potatoes, peel the strange black bits off the bendy carrots, discard the half of the red pepper with the green and brown mould, rescue the middle of the tragic leek from the squidgy outer layers, repurpose the leftover cauliflower cheese. Some sorry-looking mushrooms, a couple of onions. Three cloves of garlic. All they need is a stock gel, a can of beans (borlotti, cannellini, haricot, maybe even kidney) and a tin of tomatoes. Before you know it, you've conjured up a hearty Mediterranean bean soup with a little help from the herb-and-spice shelf.

When I was a trainee journalist on starvation wages, I used to make a vat of soup on a Sunday evening. Proper soup, with vegetables I'd chosen for the job. Leek and potato; lentil and bacon; mushroom and onion; minestrone; a trusty Scotch broth. That, plus a loaf of bread from the bakery underneath our office, kept me going till Friday and cost very little, leaving enough cash for the weekend jug of Devon farm cider.

Making big pans of soup in winter is a habit I still cleave to. It's central heating for the soul. My partner is in the other camp and she really doesn't understand what she's missing. Instead, she leans in to stews and casseroles, rich with venison, garlic, chillies, corn and chocolate, or curries from every corner of South-East Asia, or tofu, red peppers and shallots with crispy sage leaves that crack into flavour in the mouth. I love her cooking – even when it's a bottom-of-the-fridge curry – but left to my own devices, I always turn to soup.

The other staple of winter food is porridge. My grandfathers were both miners and my maternal grandfather actually did perform the weekly ritual that some people think is an urban myth. On Sunday evening, he'd make a big pot of porridge – oatmeal, water and salt – and pour it into a kitchen drawer lined with greaseproof paper. Every day he'd cut a slice, add a thin thread of golden syrup and put it in his 'piece box' along with his sandwich and take it down the pit with him.

I enjoy my porridge in the winter but I'm not as hardy as my grandfather. Purists consider this heresy, but I make my porridge with milk and assorted additions such as dried fruit, fresh berries, warming spices, nut butter and pumpkin seeds. It divides the crowd and I'm told I wouldn't be permitted to enter it for the national porridge championships. But for me, it's the breakfast of champions and the variations keep me going on those dreich winter days.

WINTER SOLSTICE

Halfway house

One of the key seasonal markers is the shortest day of the year, the winter solstice. Here in Edinburgh, the sun doesn't rise till 8.43am, then sets again less than seven hours later, at 15.39. This has been our first winter in our new home, so there's a lot of change to accommodate in our surroundings. We're enjoying the anticipation of what will emerge as the year turns.

We've already spotted the sturdy rosemary bush near the front door and the substantial bay tree at the end of the top bed. I have them earmarked for inclusion in the festive game stew of venison, wild boar and rabbit; there will be more herbs next year – a sage plantation, lemon thyme, a curry plant, maybe even some chillies – but these two will do for now.

This past solstice, before sunrise, the sky lightened in the east, pallid at first then brightening to the colour of a robin's egg. The forecast was for rain but it wasn't very forthcoming, just scant blustery scatters of droplets, not enough to deter the planting out of a couple of new trees – a *Magnolia stellata*, with its promise of delicate flowers much more varied in colour than the ubiquitous flat paint shades, and a crab apple, whose fruit will appear like jewels in the early autumn.

The new town planners who designed Glenrothes in Fife in the 1950s laid out the streets with grass verges between the pavements and the roads. In the grass verges, they planted dozens of crab apple trees. But most people didn't know what to do with the sour, bitter fruit, so they'd leave them to drop to the ground and rot. But my family were great foragers of fruit.

The year's succession of fruit would run: rhubarb, wild strawberries, raspberries, blackcurrants, greengages and Victoria plums, blackberries and, finally, those unloved crab apples. My father and I would go out gathering – there was a ruined walled garden belonging to a former grand house near where we lived that always provided rich pickings. My mother and my gran would transform them into jams and jellies, boiled up in their vast preserving pans, then strained through inverted witches' hats of muslin. My job was to stick the labels on the jars once they'd been filled and cooled. They were distributed round friends and family at Christmas or donated to church bazaars.

Next year, I'll pick ours when they ripen and, in my gran's old jeely pan, I'll make crab apple jelly, the perfect accompaniment to roast meat and strong cheese.

ROAMING IN THE GLOAMING

THIS PAST YEAR, AS THE SOLSTICE APPROACHED, THERE were some spectacular skies, particularly around sunset – streaks of gold, russet, vermilion, purple and scarlet, with backdrops of pearl white or the bright blue of Renaissance paintings. The glamour of the changing light as the day slipped into night via the gloaming was breathtaking. It was almost worth the seasonal early darkness.

The most striking gloaming experience I had this year came thanks to a diversion en route to delivering the Christmas lecture for the Leverhulme Centre for Forensic Science at Dundee University. I have a long-standing relationship with the scientists attached to the centre and I was flattered to be asked, as a writer of fiction, to speak about the very real science my friends do there. I'd chosen as my subject 'The Unforeseen Consequences of Developments in Forensic Science'. I hadn't considered I might encounter my own unforeseen consequences on the journey.

The motorway north was closed for repairs and we were diverted down the byways of North Fife. It's a route with few settlements, so the skies are dark, the stars bright and that evening, the moon that rose was full. We'd just endured a couple of days and nights of hard frost – a spell of weather where the temperature never rose above freezing, even in midday sunshine.

The road gleamed black in the moonlight, a dark ribbon threading through the trees and the undergrowth on either side of the road. Thanks to the thick frost covering them, the grasses, the bracken and the branches shone brilliant white like ghosts of themselves. Because we'd had a mild and wet autumn, there was more woodland marcescense than usual, and those dead leaves hung stark white on the branches like albino bats, unmoving in the still air. It felt like driving through a dreamscape, a night in Narnia absent only the talking animals. That there were almost no other cars on the road added to the otherworldly feeling.

I hadn't expected such a dreamlike drive; I was almost sorry when I emerged from the frosted vision into the mundanity of the Tay Bridge and the sparkling lights of Dundee's waterfront.

TWITCHING

WINTER BIRDS ARE MUCH EASIER TO OBSERVE ONCE THE shrubs and garden trees have shed their leaves. During the rest of the year, birdsong is a perpetual counterpoint to whatever else is going on, from the noisy dawn chorus of blackbirds, finches, assorted tits, the chattering of wrens and the crooning of wood pigeons. There's even a woodpecker who taps out a rhythm on the oaks across the road. But the canopies of trees and the foliage of garden plants obscures the birds themselves; they're the opposite of Victorian children – heard but not seen.

But in winter, it's a different story. Not least because the birds are on the constant lookout for food. In our previous house, because we lived in a relatively built-up area of Georgian houses and tenements, bird-feeding was compromised by the presence of rats. We had a specialist feeder that took stills and videos of the consumers of our offerings; imagine our shock the day a picture arrived on our phones of a very fat rat, scoffing everything in sight.

We tried spraying the pole that led to the feeder with WD40, which produced some very entertaining comedy clips of rats climbing the pole then sliding back down, again and again. In the end, we fitted a transparent dome to the top of the pole. The rats were smart enough to realise very quickly that they'd been outwitted and went elsewhere.

In our new house it was a different clan of rodents that proved problematic. We hung four feeders from the branches of a young tree near the house with a variety of treats – suet balls, peanuts, seeds, mealworms. Because we could watch the outcome from our large living room windows, we very soon observed the thuggish grey squirrels scaring the birds away and wreaking havoc. They dragged the feeders to the ground, worked together to pull the lids off and cleaned out all four feeders in an afternoon.

We didn't want to contribute to the increase of the local grey squirrel population. They don't need any encouragement to drive out the native red squirrels. Climate change has drastically reduced their hibernation period; now, instead of having a single litter every year, they're having two or even three. The much cuter red squirrels just can't compete territorially. So we worked out that if we managed to avoid inadvertently feeding the greys, the reds might just manage to cling on a little more easily. They belong here; we don't mind if they steal the bird food!

A little research online brought us to a website that claimed to have solved the problem – squirrel-proof feeders. The actual food source is in a traditional wire column, but beyond it is a second cage. Small birds can perch inside the outer cage or stretch into the middle from an outer wire. They can reach the food but the squirrels are entirely thwarted.

This morning, we sat and watched the birds feasting unmolested. Well, almost unmolested.

The robin redbreast still bullies the other small birds off the feeders, perching as close to us humans as it dares. But when it's worked its way through the mealworms, it takes off in search of other treats elsewhere.

The blue tits and great tits were not deterred by the robin for long and soon attacked the suet balls and the seeds. After all, blue tits need to eat almost their entire bodyweight in food in a short period of time. They're more active on these short winter days because they have less time to collect food before the sun goes down.

And later that day, we were rewarded for our persistence. As well as the tits, the finches, the wrens and the robin, we were treated to a whole family outing of pied

wagtails, coursing up from the burn at the bottom of the garden. They ate their fill, picked fights with no one then took off in a ragged shape towards the woods they'd come from. Now they've found us, I'm sure they'll be back.

I used to wonder where birds went in the freezing rain, sleet and snow of winter. It's hard enough for humans outside dressed for the weather, particularly when the wind is added to the equation. Surely there just aren't enough hedgerows and shrubs to go around? Our answer is raffia nesting pods, which we've hung around the garden. They're not just for the breeding season – they provide shelter from the weather. But I'm hopeful that in spring we'll hear baby birds cheeping and see their fledgling flights as they work up to joining their parents in the garden and the woodland.

THAT'S HOW THE LIGHT GETS IN

THE WINTER SOLSTICE ARRIVES JUST BEFORE CHRISTMAS, on the 21/22 December. It marks the turning of the year and that same promise – the light will come back.

It's an understanding humans have needed for thousands of years. If we want proof of that then it's there in physical form in the layout of the many prehistoric stone circles in the Scottish Highlands and islands. A classic example sits on a terrace above the River Nairn near Inverness. About a mile south of the desolate Culloden battlefield, where Bonnie Prince Charlie's army was famously routed in 1746, hidden in a grove of trees is the Clava Cairns. Viewers of the TV series *Outlander* will recognise their more recent rebranding as Craigh Na Dun. But they had already been standing there for the best part of four thousand years before that decisive April defeat of the Highland army.

Walking through the trees, you come upon the chambered tombs almost by surprise. The scale is almost shocking: the main cairn consists of a wide outer ring of stones more than twenty metres in diameter, encircling a central space five metres across. It's impossible not to be struck by the atmosphere – the air seems still, untouched by the winds that sweep across Culloden moor from the nearby Moray Firth. The structures feel alien, almost as if they'd dropped from space.

Back in the Bronze Age, these stone tombs were painstakingly built by people who had no mechanical assistance and only rudimentary tools, a remarkable feat in itself. The circular cairns sit on a raised earth platform amid strategically placed standing stones, some almost three metres tall. The cairns themselves are aligned along a south-west/north-east axis; when the sun sets on the midwinter solstice, its rays shine down the passageway into the heart of the tomb itself and illuminate the back of the chamber. It's an awesome feat.

And the builders didn't just assemble the cairns from a random collection of stones. They were deliberately arranged not only in order of size but also by colour. Towards the south-west, they chose red and pink sandstone. In the light of the setting sun at midwinter, they appear to glow red, the colour intensifying till the sun sinks and they grow dark. Conversely, the stones on the opposite side, the north-east, have seams of quartz running through them. As the sun rises at midsummer, the first thing visible in the dawn light is the sparkle and glint of the quartz. It seems these seasonal events mattered back in the Bronze Age. They were reassurance, I suppose. With no other way of measuring time, those dramatic moments must have served to remind people of the change of seasons and the need to pay attention to the next phase of the year.

Now it seems there are other ways we remind ourselves that Christmas is coming. On the last Sunday before Christmas Eve, we slept late. That may have had something to do with the friends who'd been to dinner the evening before. We'd had a lot of catching up to do – two of them live in New York so we don't have the chance to compare notes and swap gossip very often.

When I looked out of the bathroom window, I wondered whether I'd overdone the celebrations the night before. There, running through the park across the road were Santas and elves as far as I could see in either direction. From sprightly Santas in scarlet bodysuits to comfortably padded Clauses, from baby elves strapped to mothers in Santa hats to over-excited children who looked like escapees from the local panto or extras from another Hollywood saccharine seasonal offering, they just kept on coming.

Was I having some sort of *Muppet Christmas Carol* visitation of conscience? Were these a reproach or a threat? Was this my personal nightmare before Christmas?

'Oh,' my partner said, looking over my shoulder. 'It's the Santa Dash. And the Elf Dash. A charity fun run. Did you not see the posters on the coffee van?'

THE LIGHT FANTASTIC

I CONFESS I HAVE AN EMBARRASSING FONDNESS FOR THE extravaganzas of Christmas lights that now festoon the exteriors of so many homes. I know it's fashionable to sneer at their lack of taste and lack of concern for the future of the planet, but I love the expression of individualism and delight they embody. I tell myself it's all about keeping the darkness at bay, but really it's a childlike joy in the bright shiny things.

It really caught fire for me in December 1998, when I went to New Orleans for a pre-Christmas break. The friend I was visiting insisted we had to tour the annual display in Audubon Park. I'll admit, I was a little 'whatever' about it; I'd seen the Blackpool illuminations several times, the dramatic displays and tableaux adorning the Golden Mile. I didn't imagine that New Orleans could outdo that, except possibly in tackiness.

I was wrong. We paid our admission fee to drive into

Carousel Gardens and joined a slow-moving line of cars taking their time to get their money's worth. And it was worth every cent. The display was breathtaking in its beauty, its wit and charm, and its sheer scale. Strings of lights and tinsel were twined through the Spanish moss hanging from the old oak trees, local sporting teams were celebrated in the gaudy colours of their uniforms, nets of light covered the expansive canopy of tree branches, the Cajun *Night Before Christmas* animation of Santa's sleigh pulled by alligators gave a nod to the multicultural city and its swampy environs. To top them all, was Mr. Bingle, the iconic New Orleans Christmas mascot, a giant snowman who was flying through the skies long before Raymond Briggs sent his snowman walking in the air.

I was captivated, I admit it. Later, we left the car behind and walked the streets of the Faubourg Marigny, a residential neighbourhood adjacent to the French Quarter, where the residents seem to see Christmas as a personal challenge. Front lawns, porches, windows, car ports and even rooftops were festooned with lights, inflatables and plastic sculptures. Santa was everywhere. Snow White too. There were more deer than you'd find in the average deer park, though the New Orleans ones were mostly covered in glitter, which would make them easier prey for a hunter than Bambi's mother . . .

Every now and then, we'd pass a darkened house, miserable as a missing tooth in a gleaming mouth. 'Is this bah humbug?' I asked my friend. 'No,' she replied. 'It's poverty. It's got to be bad if they don't even have a plastic tree in the window.'

These days, my appetite for those lightfests that hold the darkness at bay is fed by the annual Christmas illuminations at 'the Botanics'. Every year, the Royal Botanic Garden in Edinburgh commissions international light trail makers to produce innovative and exciting displays that fill the night with coruscating brilliance, a series of gorgeous light sculptures that take their inspiration from the natural features of the trees and plants. From a hillside covered in toddler-sized scarlet candles with yellow and gold flames to pulsating streams of changing colours mimicking the intertwining roots underneath the ground, every year reveals innovative and creative imaginations at work. At a time when there's not much plant variety on display, the gardens are transformed into a wonderland.

Spectacular specimen trees that are easy to miss when everything is in full bloom are lit to their best advantage, reminding us that, like fingerprints, no two trees are identical. I know the light show has made me look again at those same trees when the leaves have changed their silhouettes, remembering the skeletons beneath their skins of green. The tragedy this year is that a scant month later, Storm Eowyn cut a swathe of destruction through the gardens, splintering so many specimens like matchwood. It grieves me that they won't recover in my lifetime.

I've pursued these light trails in pouring rain, biting wind and bitter cold, but they've never failed to raise my spirits. There's a promise there in the darkest days that the light will return and restore the gardens to their reliable glory. And in these days in the dead of winter, we need to be reminded of that promise.

CHRISTMAS DAYS

MY EARLIEST MEMORY IS SET LIKE A DIAMOND IN THE heart of winter. Christmas was coming and I'd been taken down the town on the bus to see the lights in Kirkcaldy town square. We lived on the seventh floor of the eight-storey flats in Valley Gardens, locally famous as a skyscraper, a bus ride from anything approaching the beating heart of anywhere.

I have no memory of the flat itself, though there's a vivid family legend from the day we were moving out, flitting to a less vertiginous home. I'd been strapped into my pram and wheeled out on to the balcony to prevent me getting under the feet of the removal men. When my gran came out to check on me a while later, she found me dangling from the wrong side of the balcony railings by the restraints of my pram. Somehow, I'd managed to escape the confines of the pram itself and lever myself over the four-foot-high railings. The story goes that I was still trying to wriggle free, showing no signs of distress. Without my gran's presence of mind, the world would be forty novels lighter . . .

But anyway. That December, 1957 to be precise, I was two and a half years old. And the town square was all the magic rolled out in one space. A towering Christmas tree – a *real* tree, not like our three-foot version with its metal branches and plastic needles and unmatching baubles – decked with dozens of lightbulbs, just like the ones that lit our rooms at home, except that these were different colours. Red, green, blue, yellow, orange, white, twinkling bravely in the dark Scottish winter night. My dad carried me aloft on his shoulders so I could see everything.

There were strings of fairy lights flashing their way round the square, their low wattage still enough to dazzle me. At one side of the tree, a fenced-off nativity scene. But much more exciting was the area next to it, where donated gifts had been left for 'the poor orphans' who lived behind the high walls of St Olaf's Children's Home.

The parcels were brightly wrapped and piled high, and I suspect I envied the orphans; Christmas wasn't that big a deal in Scotland in the 1950s. Before the Reformation of the church in 1560, Christmas had been a religious feast day. But the all-powerful puritanical Kirk insisted on turning its back on anything that reeked of Roman Catholicism, so the feasting was closed down. And in

1640, the Scottish Parliament passed a law to make the celebration of 'Yule vacations' actively illegal. Even baking the popular spiced and fruited Yule bread was a criminal act.

In spite of the Restoration, when Charles II was returned to the throne and celebrating Christmas returned to the English calendar, it was still frowned upon in Scotland for a long time, which is why Hogmanay and New Year celebrations in Scotland became so important. Christmas was formally and informally banned for four hundred years – it was informally celebrated for decades, with church nativity services and Christmas trees, but it wasn't made an official holiday in Scotland until 1958. I remember my dad having to work on Christmas Day right into the early 1960s, though he usually got the afternoon off.

As a child, I'd get one big present, a selection box of sweets that invariably contained at least one disappointing item (I dreaded the packet of Opal Fruits) and a stocking that included a wind-up toy of some description, a wee orange and a florin. For reasons I couldn't fathom, there would also be something pointless from my aunts – bath salts in fragrances that made me sneeze; insipid notelets so I could write a thank you for the gift itself or age-inappropriate soft toys that I'd surreptitiously regift to the next church sale.

We had to wait for my dad to come home before we could have Christmas dinner – the rare luxury of a whole roast chicken with Dad's recipe sausage and oatmeal stuffing cooked in a separate baking tin, potatoes mashed *and* roasted, carrots, Brussel sprouts cooked till they were grey and tinned peas. This feast was followed by the best bit – Christmas pudding with brandy custard. The pudding always contained silver threepennies wrapped in greaseproof paper. Finding one in your portion was supposed to guarantee good luck for an unspecified period. The coins had to be handed back, though – they were no longer legal tender and had to be saved for the New Year's clootie dumpling, from which they'd be returned again for the next year's birthday clooties. One memorable year, I gorged on so much Christmas pudding I spent Christmas night being violently sick in a basin.

That 1957 night in the town square, Santa had a grotto where you could pay to sit on his knee and get a present, but I preferred my own perch high on my dad's shoulders. The air was filled with the smell of hot dogs and the tinny sound of Christmas carols and Bing Crosby roasting chestnuts. I could hear my dad's braw tenor joining in.

Looking back through the distorted lens of memory, the trip is bookended by two vivid recollections. One is of an object that captivated me with what I now think of as its primitive charm. It was a glass-topped box, the size of a table football set. Inside, held prisoner in grooves cut in a sheet of plywood painted to resemble a heather moor with a distant castle, were a couple of dozen tiny plastic Scottish soldiers complete with bearskins and kilts, spats and red jackets, mostly with bagpipes but some with drums. When someone put a penny in the slot, they'd spring into limited life, moving back and forth while the speakers played a shrill rendition of 'Scotland the Brave'. I don't know why I loved it so but I did. I begged my dad for more and he gave in twice.

The other recollection is inextricably linked to that. Earlier that year, my dad's father had died. Pop wasn't just my grandad, he was my favourite friend. I remember sitting on his bed in what was his final illness, listening to his stories, laughing at his jokes, wanting to go down the pit when I was grown up, just like he had. He made it sound fun, days underground with his pals. I loved Pop.

Then, suddenly, he was gone. It made no sense to me. Why would Jesus want Pop? And if Jesus got to come back at Christmas, why not Pop?

I sat that night on my dad's shoulders, sobbing that I wanted Pop. All the magic and it wasn't enough to burn out the cold, dark coal of grief in a small child's heart.

THE TURNING
OF THE YEAR

A GUID NEW YEAR
TAE YIN AN' A'

HOGMANAY REMAINS THE SIGNATURE SCOTTISH FESTIVAL in the eyes of the outside world. But the traditional New Year celebration only exists nowadays in the black and white line drawings of 'The Broons' (in English, 'the Browns'), a cartoon strip that has appeared in the *Sunday Post* since 1936. The extended family Broon have lived unchanged at 10 Glebe Street, Auchenshoogle, since then. They are possibly the last family in Scotland who cleave strictly to the Hogmanay traditions that were only just clinging on in my own childhood. For the rest of us, most of those customs have faded away.

On Auld Year's Day, the last day of the year, the house had to be cleaned. My father, and most of the men and boys we knew, had their hair cut. We children were sent to bed for a nap in the afternoon so we could stay up to handsel in the new year. We all washed – bathed if we had a bath – and put on our best clothes. We'd gather in the living room as midnight approached, the TV on to make sure we didn't miss the countdown to the bells. There was invariably something tartan-and-shortbread Scottish on the TV – the kilted dancers of the White Heather Club; Andy Stewart gurning 'Donald, Where's Your Troosers?', while my father grumbled that anyone who sang that flat shouldn't be on the telly; Jimmy Shand and his accordion band playing 'Bluebell Polka' while my grandfather reminded us yet again how he'd known Jimmy since they were young lads; Moira Anderson and Kenneth McKellar doing the proper Scottish songs; comedian Rikki Fulton satirising Scottish Presbyterianism in the shape of the Reverend I. M. Jolly. I have no idea what the English were watching; it was absolutely a foreign country for one night of the year.

Glasses were charged – whisky for the men, sherry for the women (apart from Gran who liked an advocaat and lemonade with a glacé cherry), non-alcoholic ginger wine for the children, all ready for the toast. And then the countdown to midnight. We all chanted along with the TV and then it was 'Happy New Year!' and glasses chinked all around. We embraced each other, wishing everyone in the room all the best for the coming year.

We sipped our drinks, gasping at the spiciness of the ginger wine, waiting eagerly to discover who would be our First Foot – a friend or neighbour knocking on the door, first across the threshold to bring the house good luck in the coming months. Tradition demanded they be dark and ideally handsome. Dark, allegedly because there was still a race memory of blond or red-haired Vikings, who definitely did not mean good luck. One year, I first-footed old friends. I was neither dark nor handsome enough, and I was blamed for every misfortune that befell them that year. I'm still not sure whether they were entirely joking.

Tradition also demanded that the First Foots had to bring their own bottle of whisky, which they'd pass around the room, having their own glasses filled in return with the hosts' drink. They were also supposed to carry a lump of coal to symbolise fuel to get the household through the winter and something to eat, usually short-bread or the much-dreaded (in my view) black bun. The black bun is like a Garibaldi biscuit on steroids – a large pastry case filled with dried fruit and candied peel. All I remember of them from my childhood is an excess of currants that made it feel like chewing a mouthful of soil.

First Foots would come and go as the night passed. As the drink flowed, the grown-ups would take turns to deliver their party piece, songs and poems hefted to their individual performers. Heaven forfend a stranger should turn up and attempt a piece that 'belonged' to another. I can still remember the glacial silence that greeted an interloper's rendition of my father's earmarked New Year special, 'The Road and the Miles to Dundee'. Sometimes, if the room was big enough, there would be a chaotic attempt at Scottish country dancing; once, after a particularly violent Strip the Willow, I was literally bruised from shoulder to knee!

But over the past thirty years or so, these traditions have ebbed away. Large-scale celebrations in town and city centres, special dinners in restaurants, late licences in clubs and bars have replaced those domestic events that now feel quaint in the memory. In the capital, for example, we have Edinburgh's 'Hogmanay!', a giant street party with live music, spectacular fireworks and thousands of people celebrating with all the stops out. Some streets in the city are closed off for days in advance to facilitate the event; I'll admit to being grumpy that I'm forced to make extensive detours to walk across the centre of my own city. Some residents need to have a special permit to get to and from their own residences in the absence of an expensive ticket for the celebrations, effectively forbidden from having private parties in their homes.

Yes, the fireworks are visible from miles away, but the street party that used to be spontaneous and free-flowing around Princes Street and its gardens is no more. To be fair, it's not just in the Hogmanay capital of the world that the festivities have been turned into expensive corporate and heavily restricted events. It's the same story in London and other major cities in the UK and around the world. Public shared spaces once open to all are contracted out by many local authorities to private companies.

We're told it's for our own safety. That unfettered crowds will turn barbaric under the influence of the festive spirit, both literal and metaphorical. We need to gather in closed spaces like sports stadia or concert arenas. We sit in our assigned seats or standing areas. Sometimes we are turned away if we're not in place in time.

But I do mourn the random gatherings at Hogmanay. In Kirkcaldy, people would gather spontaneously in the town square to count down to the New Year. It was a chance to run into old school friends and former neighbours, to greet strangers without fear. We'd wish each other a happy New Year and, if we knew them well enough, swap swigs from our New Year bottles. There was always some sort of musical entertainment and a small-scale firework display funded by the local council. A wee bit of chaotic dancing and everyone linking arms for 'Auld Lang Syne' topped off the celebration.

Now, there's nothing. The town square stands empty and unwelcoming. People pass each other in the town centre in awkward silence with eyes averted. It's as if the square's been turned into a space we no longer have a common claim over. And that makes me sad. American writer and activist Barbara Ehrenreich said, 'The urge to transform one's appearance, to dance outdoors, to mock the powerful and embrace perfect strangers is not easy to suppress.' But suppressed it has largely been.

To be honest, we've given up on Edinburgh at New Year. Instead, we decamp to a fishing village in the East Neuk of Fife, where a crowd assembles down by the harbour with their bottles and glasses for the countdown to the bells. We cheer our small firework display and hope for a clear night so we can see across the Forth to the pyrotechnics at Edinburgh and other towns along the East Lothian coast. One of the neighbours keeps open house and it's a cosy approximation of a traditional gathering.

This year, when the Edinburgh 'Hogmanay!' celebrations were cancelled at the last minute because weather forecasters predicted gales and torrential rain, part of me hoped that people would rock up anyway and have an impromptu street party. Especially after the weather gods produced a late reprieve: the wind dropped substantially and the rain eased. But only a few people turned up on Princes Street. Either they'd swiftly made other plans – in which case, good for them – or they'd lost their nerve for taking a chance on becoming part of an arms-open-wide kind of celebration among strangers. And that makes me even more sad.

*

Nevertheless, I have to confess to making my own contribution to Edinburgh's New Year festivities. A few years ago, the decision was taken to extend the celebration from Hogmanay to Burns Night with *Message from the Skies: New Year's Resurrection* – a *son et lumière* spectacular across twelve sites in the city centre. I was invited to create the narrative for a walk that would reveal an unfamiliar element of the city's literary history.

As I struggled for a theme, I remembered a novel I'd stumbled across many years previously, when I was an undergraduate at Oxford – *Marriage* by Susan Ferrier. It wasn't part of the main syllabus, but I'd read a reference to it and wondered whether there were any Scottish women publishing novels at the same time as the big names – Austen, the Brontës, George Eliot. *Marriage* is a vivid and entertaining novel, a social comedy with many of the elements that made Jane Austen so popular. An aspect Austen lacks that Ferrier exploited to the full was life below stairs – the book is more *Downton Abbey* than *Bridgerton*!

I wondered why Susan Ferrier had failed to make the literary canon and started to do a little digging. My first discovery was that she was born in 1782 in an apartment in Lady Stair's Close, a courtyard off the Royal Mile in Edinburgh that now houses the city's Writer's Museum – a building that honours Robert Burns, Sir Walter Scott and Robert Louis Stevenson. Not Susan Ferrier, nor any other women writers. It's as if Muriel Spark never put pen to paper . . .

Ferrier was privately educated and her family moved in the upper echelons of Edinburgh society. Her closest friend was Charlotte Clavering, a granddaughter of the Duke of Argyll, and Ferrier was a regular visitor to the home of Sir Walter Scott, who praised her as the equal of other successful women contemporaries such as Maria Edgeworth and Fanny Burney. Her books outsold Jane Austen, her advances exceeded Austen's and *Marriage* was translated successfully into French, while *Pride and Prejudice* only appeared as a pirated edition in France.

The more I found out, the more possibilities offered themselves to me for locations. And so, on 1 January, a freezing cold Ne'erday night with sleet blowing in from the Forth, *New Year's Resurrection* opened in Parliament Square, outside St Giles' Cathedral, with my dramatic message from Susan Ferrier, projected on the Signet Library:

When I was six years old, my daddy took me to see a man being hanged, right where you're standing now. Half the city was here. Forty thousand people turned up to see Deacon Brodie swing from a gallows tree he'd designed himself. A proper eighteenth century gentleman, or so everybody thought.

But somehow, in a small city where houses crowded close and people knew every noisy detail of their neighbours' lives, Brodie managed to keep his secrets. Not a single member of the Edinburgh establishment was aware that he had not one, but two mistresses who between them had given birth to five of his children.

It takes a lot of money to keep a secret as big as that. Brodie's answer was simple. He was the city locksmith. So he made extra copies of the keys that unlocked the doors of the rich and comfortable. And in the night, he crept into their homes and their offices and robbed the very citizens he rubbed shoulders with in business and politics. When they discovered how he'd bamboozled them, there was only ever going to be one outcome.

I saw Deacon Brodie's last dance from my daddy's shoulders. Maybe you think that's a terrible thing to show a child. But that's Edinburgh for you. Don't be fooled by the superficial charms. Edinburgh is as ruthless as she is lovely. Here, now, at the turning of the year, when Janus-faced January looks to the past as well as the future, we're held fast in the frosty embrace of Edinburgh. This is a city of opposites. Good and evil. Old and new. High life and low life. Respectable . . . and very definitely unrespectable. But most of all, it's a city of stories.

My story shifted round the corner to the National Library of Scotland, where the message read:

Welcome to Edinburgh, UNESCO City of Literature. Home to Sir Walter Scott, Robert Burns, Sir Arthur Conan Doyle, Robert Louis Stevenson and—

The message was then interrupted by a single word: *ENOUGH!*

And we were off, on a journey round the city with Susan as our guide. From Lady Stair's Close to the Bank of Scotland, where the view of the Scott Monument was hijacked, replacing the statue of Sir Walter with one of Susan, to the Scotsman Steps, where the walls were adorned with the names of Scottish women writers, past the Conan Doyle pub and Robert Louis Stevenson's childhood home. We passed the Ferrier family grave, a dramatic pair of carved stone Gothic arches. Finally, to celebrate her centenary year, Muriel Spark took over as tour guide, leading us through the Grassmarket to

Greyfriars churchyard, which was illuminated with a series of neon signs celebrating great Scottish writers, past and present, men and women. Thousands of people braved the cruel Edinburgh temperature to walk the winter streets. It was exhilarating, even on a freezing January night, especially with the atmospheric sound-scape of acoustic music and electronic effects, and an amazing experience to be part of.

*

The last night of that New Year's Resurrection was, appropriately, 25 January – Burns Night. The birthday of our national bard is celebrated all round the globe, from Miami to Moscow. People gather together to share a Burns Supper – the traditional menu of haggis, neeps and tatties washed down with a wee dram (trans: sheep's offal cooked in a sheep's stomach with oatmeal and spices, including a lot of white pepper; mashed swede/rutabaga; mashed potatoes; a glass of whisky). The haggis arrives on a large salver, preceded by a man in a kilt playing the bagpipes.

Then the haggis is addressed. Yes, really. 'To a Haggis', the Burns poem declaimed over its steaming girth speaks directly to its legendary qualities. It's stabbed with a sharp knife or sword before it's dished up. The meal is followed by speeches – the Toast to the Lassies, the Reply on Behalf of the Lassies (which used always to be delivered by a man because many Burns Suppers did not permit the presence of any except serving women) and finally the Toast to the Immortal Memory of Robert Burns.

When I gave the Immortal Memory at the Annual Mixed Supper of the Bowhill People's Burns Club in 2023, I was the first woman to do so. Their first Burns Supper was convened in 1940 by members of the Bowhill Communist Party, many of them miners, shipyard and railway workers, all of them male, and the organisation has always had a strong backbone of members who take their Burns scholarship seriously and respect his philosophy of internationalism.

As I stood up, there was a definite air of tension in the room – would I be able to live up to past speakers such as Edwin Morgan, Hugh MacDiarmid, Norman MacCaig and Lib Dem Leader Charlie Kennedy?

I was not afraid for I know I owe so much to my father's love of Burns' work, particularly his songs. For years, my father was the lead tenor in the club's concert party – no mean feat when between them, the club's hundred members can perform over sixty poems or songs from the bard's repertoire. Over the winter months, the concert party would turn out to provide the entertainment at dozens of Burns Suppers throughout the region. As a result, I grew up with Burns' songs ringing in my ears, their words as familiar to me as nursery rhymes.

Through those lines, I absorbed many of the tenets that have shaped my attitudes and beliefs. From 'A Man's a Man for a' That', I learned I was as good as anyone else, that respect is earned not bought, and that I should call no one my master. From 'A Parcel o' Rogues' I discovered that the Act of Union between Scotland and England was very far from universally accepted as a fair bargain. From 'Holy Willie's Prayer' I came to understand how rich was the seam of hypocrisy in religious and public life. From 'Ae Fond Kiss' I realised the power of love thwarted. And in so many of the poems, I recognised the importance of standing shoulder to shoulder with my fellow human beings against exploitation and inhumanity.

So every January, those tenets are reinforced as I spend at least one evening celebrating the genius that is Burns. I've spoken at the LGBT Burns Supper in New York; I've sung 'Green Grow the Rashes' in St Petersburg; I've held strangers' hands and sung 'Auld Lang Syne' in more places than I can count. For me, every year, those cold January nights signal an opportunity for reinvigoration

and resurrection. Not least in the opening stanza of this
Burns poem:

> While Europe's eye is fix'd on mighty things,
> The fate of Empires and the fall of Kings;
> While quacks of State must each produce his plan,
> And even children lisp the Rights of Man;
> Amid this mighty fuss just let me mention,
> The Rights of Woman merit some attention.

WINTER SPORTS

IT'S GRATIFYING TO ME THAT WE CAN STILL INVENT NEW traditions. One of these is the Loony Dook. Officially, it began in 1986 in South Queensferry, a burgh west of Edinburgh on the coast of the Firth of Forth. A trio of locals dared each other to cure their New Year's Day hangovers with a dook – or plunge – into the bitter sea at the end of the old harbour mole. For some reason, this Ne'erday adventure caught on and by the early 1990s, it had been christened the Loony Dook. The organisers invite the dookers to make donations for charity.

As if it wasn't enough for participants to hurl themselves into the shockingly cold water, the new tradition expanded into a fancy dress challenge. Now dookers parade through the town, past the Hawes Inn (said to be the place that inspired Robert Louis Stevenson to say, 'Some places speak distinctly. Certain dark gardens cry aloud for a murder; certain old houses demand to be haunted; certain coasts are set apart for shipwreck'). They're greeted by bagpipers and locals with bowls of porridge to fortify and energise them.

The rise in popularity of 'wild swimming' – or 'swimming', as we used to call it when I was a child learning breaststroke in those same waters – has caused the concept of the Ne'erday Loony Dook to spread far beyond its original home. On the other side of the Forth, all along the East Neuk of Fife, dookers can take their pick of a variety of locations. From the tidal pools of St Monans and Pittenweem to the harbour at Anstruther and the East Sands at St Andrews, there is no shortage of hardy souls braving the elements and the goose pimples to greet the New Year. There are New Year plunges on the west coast too and even in England! Me, I wrap up warmly and applaud . . .

*

The winter of 1963 is engraved on my memory like the lines my skates left in the ice. We had snow like no other winter I'd known. Growing up on the east coast of Scotland, we were always told the winter weather came straight to us from the Urals. I had no idea then what the Urals were, except that they must be freezing. My mother said we all had such lovely skin because the vicious east winds exfoliated us on a daily basis.

That winter was particularly bitter. Snow came swirling down in thick, heavy flakes. Our teacher, Hammy Bones Hamilton, made us learn Robert Bridges' poem 'London Snow'. I fell in love with the words. I can still pull those opening lines out of memory.

> When men were all asleep the snow came flying,
> In large white flakes falling on the city brown,
> Stealthily and perpetually settling and loosely lying,
> Hushing the latest traffic of the drowsy town;
> Deadening, muffling, stifling its murmurs failing;
> Lazily and incessantly floating down and down:
> Silently sifting and veiling road, roof and railing;
> Hiding difference, making unevenness even,
> Into angles and crevices softly drifting and sailing.

I can still recall it because it seemed to me, even at that early age, to capture exactly the feeling of a blanket of snow muffling all the sounds of the town, transforming the landscape, making everything fresh and clean.

One year, there was a bus strike and we had to walk back from our high school, three miles away at the back of the town where the snow was deepest. By the time we got home it was dark, my shoes and socks were sodden and I couldn't feel my feet. Next day, I wore my wellies and thick hockey socks. Nothing says 'Scotland in winter' like walking to school with dawn barely broken, then walking back in the dark . . .

Nowadays children are hastily sent home from school as soon as a few flakes fall, for fear they'll be trapped in the classroom. But when I was wee, there were no such things as 'snow days' when schools were closed down. It never crossed anyone's mind that we should skip school because of the weather. And so in that 1963 winter, we had to wait till Saturday for a full-on assault on the snowscape.

With my skates slung round my neck, my dog at my side, a couple of pals from the street and the posh boy from Carlyle Road we tolerated because he had a proper wooden sledge, we trooped along the slush-bordered pavements to the park. Kirkcaldy is bookended by two impressive public parks. To the east, Ravenscraig Park runs along the rocky coast from the ruins of the eponymous fifteenth-century castle, the first in Scotland built to withstand cannon fire. At the other end of the park, a path passes through woodland to the picturesque Dysart harbour. Ravenscraig tended to be a summer destination; twice a month on Sundays, the bandstand would host a free concert from a brass or silver band, performing a wide repertoire from popular classical music to film themes. My parents loved the concerts; I enjoyed them when I was small but mostly I looked forward either to the greaseproof bag of crisps with its tiny square, blue bag of salt for shaking over or the bliss of a wafer cone filled with Scottish vanilla ice cream, a flavour as regionally specific as Camembert or champagne.

To the west, Beveridge Park was closer to home and boasted a boating lake complete with a tiny island and, among the plentiful waterfowl, a single black swan. She had been christened Jenny by the park authorities, which seemed to me a name whose dullness was incompatible with her exoticism. In my head, I made up tales of her dramatic escape to safety from some foreign oppression involving men with scimitars and women with elegantly carved longbows. In our humble park, Jenny had found sanctuary, the very ordinariness of her name an effective disguise against her enemies. What can I say? It was symptomatic of my growing belief that the world of my imagination might actually exist beyond my head, that if I could only spread my wings wide enough I might reach escape velocity and find it.

That winter almost convinced me. There was proper snow, just like a Hans Christian Andersen story. And the park pond froze over. Not a thin skin of cat-ice that would creak and splinter and break, but the real thing – thick, opaque, load-bearing. It didn't even give at the margins. It wasn't as smooth as the ice rink, but it wasn't too hard to navigate the bumpy bits.

My parents had encouraged me to frequent the local ice rink, perhaps because it had been at the heart of their courtship. They used to go skating together, whirling round the rink on Saturday nights when there was no ice hockey match, then sitting in the café drinking hot chocolate till it was time for my dad to walk my mum to the stop where she could catch the last bus home. Their association of good times with the ice rink meant they'd bought me skates of my own, rather than renting them by the session.

At the park pond that winter, while the others took tentative steps on to the ice then struggled to keep their balance, feet scampering like cartoon characters, I struck out boldly, not quite graceful but not quite comedic either. My buddies stumbled back to the path, a couple of them on their knees, staring at me as I got into a rhythm I'd perfected at the ice rink. I was a long way off Henry Raeburn's striking portrait of the Reverend Robert Walker skating on Duddingston Loch – apart from anything else, my arms were working hard to give me balance, unlike Walker's, folded elegantly across his chest – but in my mind, compared to my pals, I was giving Jenny the swan a run for her money. I managed a circuit of the islet without falling and made it back to my friends, stopping with a spray of ice crystals from the serrated tip of one blade.

The respect lasted until I failed to steer the posh boy's sledge in a straight line down the hill, hit a bump, took off and face-planted into the snow as the sledge carried on without me. That shock of snow down the inside of my anorak and the gleeful laughter of my pals restored the usual order of things. But it didn't take away the remembered thrill of whizzing over the ice with the wind singing in my ears, the cold bringing tears of joy to my eyes. Even though I can never repeat it on my older and shoogly legs, I can still recall that exhilarating heat of excitement and confidence. Only in winter . . .

ESCAPE

IN JANUARY, EDINBURGH IS AT ITS MOST GREY. BREATH clouding in front of our frozen faces, we climb the steep hill from the bottom of the New Town up icy pavements, feet skidding on granite setts as we cross the streets, grateful for red lights at junctions so we can catch our breath. But it's worth it. For not all winter pleasures require staying outside in the freezing cold. In Edinburgh, January lays on a breathtaking treat for art lovers, all the more delightful because it happens indoors, inside the National Gallery of Scotland, an imposing neoclassical building at the foot of the Mound, hard by Princes Street.

Henry Vaughan inherited a substantial fortune in 1830 at the tender age of twenty-one; in what feels like a very nineteenth-century success story, the Vaughans made their pile from making hats. (Incidentally, they were probably responsible for a significant number of inmates in insane asylums; the mercury used in the industrial process literally drove the hatmakers crazed, hence the expression 'mad as a hatter'.)

Clearly, Henry didn't work in the factory; rather than being condemned to a Victorian madhouse, he fell in love with art and became a discerning connoisseur and collector. He spent his inheritance living the life of a wealthy leisured gentleman, travelling across the great cities of Europe acquiring artworks as he went. He was rich enough to build a collection based around the drawings of painters such as Michelangelo, Raphael, Rubens and Rembrandt, as well as work by his contemporaries. It was those Victorian artists who came to dominate his interests; among his acquisitions was John Constable's *The Hay Wain*, which he presented to the National Gallery in London as an act of philanthropy. His home was filled with paintings and sculptures, tapestries and stained glass – an eclectic collection of opulent beauty.

And then there was Joseph Mallord William Turner – by any measure, one of the greatest painters of the nineteenth century. He had the remarkable ability to create work that speaks both to those who understand his technical brilliance and to those who don't know much about art but know instinctively what they like. I was one of those; all I knew about art was what I had been exposed to in the local art gallery in Kirkcaldy. I was lucky – the gallery has an excellent collection of the Scottish Colourists, which prepared me for what lay ahead.

As a student, I used to bunk off to London whenever I could scrounge a lift. I didn't go for the shops or the night life – I went for the art galleries. Well, they were free . . . And I discovered Turner. Unlike Henry Vaughan, I couldn't afford to buy artworks. But the world has moved on since Henry was falling in love with beautiful paintings. Now, it was possible for someone like me to buy prints from those national collections to attach to my college room walls.

Rail, Steam and Speed – The Great Western Railway and *The Fighting Temeraire tugged to her last berth to be broken up, 1838*, accompanied me through my university career and beyond, along with Botticelli's *Portrait of a Young Man* and Paolo Uccello's *Saint George and the Dragon*. Their presence lifted my spirits and often calmed me after a difficult day.

Like lots of major collectors, Henry Vaughan was interested in meeting the creators of the work he bought. He was clearly a fan – by the time they met, probably around 1840, he'd already started amassing a collection of drawings and watercolours that covered Turner's entire sixty-year career. Unlike many obsessives, Henry wasn't a completist – he was only interested in the very best of Turner's output.

I like to think of the pair of them meeting – Henry shy and polite, Turner unsure of whether this enthusiasm was uncritical fanboying or a judicious appreciation of the work, the pair of them metaphorically circling each other, trying to find the right footing for their relationship.

However that meeting went, it cemented Henry's commitment to Turner's work. And every January, we can feast on thirty-eight of his finest watercolour sketches, thanks to the terms of Henry's bequest. It states that the works should be exhibited 'to the public all at one time, free of charge, during the month of January', because in that month, the weak hours of daylight are minimal and the works can be safely exhibited without risk of them being faded or damaged. For the rest of the year, they're kept in a closed cabinet in the gallery's Print Room.

But the National Gallery of Scotland understands that not everyone who wants to see the Turners can make a pilgrimage to Edinburgh. And so they've created an online gallery where anyone with digital access can enjoy the Henry Vaughan Bequest. It's here: https://www.national galleries.org/art-and-artists/collections/vaughan-bequest. I like to think Henry would approve of the opportunity to share his favourite artist with a wider audience. And because of the power of the digital, it's possible to zoom in to the point where the very brushstrokes are visible. To any aspiring watercolourist, it's a bit of a masterclass. And not just in January.

For me, the Turners represent confidence in the light coming back. Maybe because of those two prints whose brilliant colours lifted my spirits for years, pinned to a succession of bedroom walls when I clung to the dream that one day I'd be a writer. So nowadays, that annual pilgrimage to the watercolours reminds me of the power of dreaming, of holding fast to ambition even when its realisation seems against the odds.

THE END IS NIGH . . .

AND AS THE YEAR MOVES FORWARD, SO DOES THIS
year's book. The days grow longer and the book does
too. But just like the winter weather, it doesn't proceed in
a straight line. A few days of sunshine, then a cold snap
that stops growth in its tracks. A thick fog that descends
out of nowhere, deceptive glimmers of light emerging
then fading back to disappointing gloom. A startling
sunset, then blankets of fine rain that chill the very soul.
But when everything seems hopeless, the improbable
green pushes through the dark soil.

First, the snowdrops, fragile and delicate. Back in Fife,
their return is celebrated in the Scottish Snowdrop Festival,
which runs from the end of January to the middle of March
at the Cambo Estate near Kingsbarns in the East Neuk. It's
the Plant Heritage national collection of snowdrops; just as
crime fiction comes in many shapes and sizes, so the snowdrops have more than two hundred varieties.

There are so many swathes and banks of snowdrops that their leaves green the ground in miraculous contrast to the colours of soil and leaf mould. The woodland walk winds through bare trunks and evergreens, but everywhere the eye is drawn to those nodding white heads until eventually we emerge on the Fife Coastal Path, where the inhospitable North Sea reminds us we're still firmly in the grip of winter.

But once the snowdrops stick their heads above the parapet, they're soon followed by other stark warnings to winter that the end is nigh. Dwarf irises appear overnight, their blue and purple always a sudden arrival with no apparent advance indication. Then the grape hyacinths, the bright blue stars of the chionodoxa, the multicoloured spreads of crocuses and the miniature daffodils. And my favourites, the snake's head fritillaries that feel to me as if they've dropped in from another planet where plants are scarily sentient beings.

All of the colours of the spring bulbs are the heralds of the green canopy of the trees, the final evidence that the light always comes back.

As the days start to stretch past the spring equinox, so my book stretches for the final straight. Another winter past, another book added to the shelf. This winter may now be history but there will be others. For me, that means another season of creativity. And so I celebrate the

end of the winter festivals because it promises not just the light returning but also that the darkness will come back to be illuminated by words.

Acknowledgements

Writing this book has been a welcome opportunity to delve into my memories of winters past and my appreciation of winters present. So I owe a debt of gratitude to Kirty Topiwala at Hodder for offering me the chance to depart from my usual gig of murderous fiction. Thanks also to Lucy Buxton, Becca Mundy and Laura Sherlock for all the backroom support.

So much of my experience of the changing seasons and their assorted gifts came from my parents and my maternal grandparents. I was fortunate to grow up sandwiched between seaside and woodlands, and to be encouraged to explore both. My grandfather was a miner, and he seized every chance to get out in the open air, and I was always happy to be at his heels. He knew the names of all the trees, the different shells on the beach, the succession of wildflowers that bloomed in the woods and on the shores. I remain perpetually grateful for that grounding. I couldn't have done this without them.

Kudos too to the Royal Botanic Gardens in Edinburgh, the National Gallery in Edinburgh and the Cambo Estate, home to the Plant Heritage national collection of snowdrops for the delight they variously give me during the season.

Let's all raise a glass to the joys of winter!

About the Illustrator

Philip Harris is an an illustrator and printmaker based in Devon. His work is inspired by nature, history and folklore, often reflecting the diverse landscapes of his home county. He uses traditional techniques, such as dip pen and ink and linocut, influenced by the art materials he inherited from his grandfather.

Winter is an especially inspirational season for Philip; there is something incredibly evocative about the skeletal trees atop the hillside or the winter storm that howls and batters the coastline. The season offers a glimpse of nature in a beautifully bleak state.

THE SEASONS SERIES

Winter is part of a landmark series of non-fiction books about the seasons written by some of Britain's most celebrated fiction writers.

Winter sits alongside *Spring* by Michael Morpurgo, *Summer* by Bernardine Evaristo and *Autumn* by Kate Mosse. Each book reflects the distinct voice and approach of its writer.

Leave the cold of winter behind and turn the page for a glimpse into Michael Morpurgo's bestselling story of *Spring*.

MARCH

The vernal equinox

THERE IS SNOW ON THE HIGH TORS OF DARTMOOR THIS morning. Mountains of clouds are building up over the moor and coming our way. I know it is spring because it is the vernal equinox, and because snowdrops and daffodils and primroses are everywhere. So, it must be officially spring. But it isn't. I know what spring should be and this isn't it.

I live in deepest Devon, between Dartmoor and Exmoor. It is remote and rural, so we can't ignore the weather or the seasons. As tide and wind determine the lives of sailors, so, as country people, farming folk, the seasons determine ours. They determine our lives, to some extent, wherever we live.

I have lived my life mostly in the countryside in England, with occasional forays into town and city. And I am lucky enough to have spent the last fifty or so years living on a farm down a deep lane with high hedges on either side, a lane of potholes and puddles, with grass growing down the middle, a lane that leads only to the River Torridge, which borders the farm, a lane that is fast degrading, becoming a track. As Kipling might have put it, 'Weather and rain have undone it again, / And now you would never know / There once was a road . . .'

Fifty years ago now, I wrote a diary of my first year living down this lane, my first year of working on the land, of farming; I think it was the first year I had really noticed the seasons. It became a book (one of my earliest books). I called it *All Around the Year*. There is a poem by Ted Hughes for each month, with photographs by James Ravilious and drawings by his wife, Robin Ravilious. We were neighbours, all of them better versed than I was in the countryside and in the seasons.

Little has changed. Seasons come and seasons go. They create the pace of our lives, a unifying element for all of us who live here. We see nature and the countryside and farming much as our predecessors did, we live in the same rhythm as they did. We share this place with them, live the same seasons.

We understand what Thomas Hardy meant by 'the old association', that link we forge by living in the footsteps of those who have farmed and lived off the land around us for centuries before us, who made the cottages we live in, who fished the rivers, built and grew the hedges, who planted the trees, who walked where we walk, saw the otters, the herons, the slow worms, the hedgehogs, the rabbits, the foxes and the badgers, who longed for spring as we do, for the sun to warm our backs, for the trees to bud, the grass and corn to grow.

Our work demands that we live much of our lives outside. We like it that way, that's why we are here, why we stay here. It is a difficult place to live in many ways. Everything, except the countryside, is far away – the hospital, the doctor, the shops, the cinema, the swimming pool, the theatre. Satnav often can't find us, and we like that. There are more potholes in our lane than in all the rest of Devon. Only a slight exaggeration.

My wife and I live in a small cottage, built about three hundred years ago. It's a two-up two-down farm worker's cottage. The farm that has been our life, and the lives of our predecessors here, is all around us. They built the cottage of stones gathered from the fields round about, with thick cob walls made of hardened mud and straw – and pigs' blood sometimes, I am told. It has the smallest of windows to keep out the cold, and a thatched roof to keep the place cool in summer and warm in winter.

So, this cottage has become paradise to us, familiar, a place full of memories, of history. Before we lived here, the family pig lived in part of the house, in our kitchen. Years ago, centuries ago, there was a door for the pig and a door for the farm worker and his family.

SPRING

We knew the old lady, Miss Dovey, who lived here just before us, who had an outside toilet, and lived her evenings in a tent in the living room, because the place leaked so much. We know there was a young lad born in this cottage, who went off down the lane in 1914 to the First World War and never came back. We are conscious that this place has not been paradise for everyone. There was and there is poverty down these deep lanes. We are the lucky generation. The cottage is our hive, our work-place and our home too. We've made it warm and dry, a tea cosy of a place.

Like those who have lived here before us, there are mornings when we hardly have to look out of the window to know how it is outside. When rain thunders down on the roof and lashes at the windows, it's best not to look out. A rhyme from childhood keeps coming to mind. 'Rain, rain, go away, come again another day!' The wind can be constant, from the south-west, not bringing the hoped-for sweet rains of spring, but still fiercer and colder than we'd like.

We idolise spring, of course, because we long for it so much during the dark cold months of winter.

Spring *by Michael Morpurgo is available now.*

RAISING READERS
Books Build Bright Futures

Dear Reader,

We'd love your attention for one more page to tell you about the crisis in children's reading, and what we can all do.

Studies have shown that reading for fun is the **single biggest predictor of a child's future life chances** – more than family circumstance, parents' educational background or income. It improves academic results, mental health, wealth, communication skills, ambition and happiness.[1]

The number of children reading for fun is in rapid decline. Young people have a lot of competition for their time. In 2024, 1 in 10 children and young people in the UK aged 5 to 18 did not own a single book at home.[2]

Hachette works extensively with schools, libraries and literacy charities, but here are some ways we can all raise more readers:

- Reading to children for just 10 minutes a day makes a difference
- Don't give up if children aren't regular readers – there will be books for them!
- Visit bookshops and libraries to get recommendations
- Encourage them to listen to audiobooks
- Support school libraries
- Give books as gifts

There's a lot more information about how to encourage children to read on our website: **www.RaisingReaders.co.uk**

Thank you for reading.

hachette UK

---

[1] National Literacy Trust, Book Ownership in 2024, November 2024
https://nlt.cdn.ngo/media/documents/Book_ownership_in_2024

[2] OECD. 2021. 21st-century readers: developing literacy skills in a digital world. Paris, France: OECD Publishing.
https://www.oecd.org/en/publications/21st-century-readers_a83d84cb-en.html